Happy Cooking ♡

CANDICE BROWN

Happy Cooking

EASY UPLIFTING MEALS AND COMFORTING TREATS

EBURY
PRESS

INTRODUCTION 6

Quick pick-me-ups 12

—

Simple comforts 48

—

Keep-your-hands-busy cooking 82

—

Food that takes care of itself (and you) 134

—

Nostalgia food 158

—

Say it with cake 198

NOTES 240

INDEX 248

ACKNOWLEDGEMENTS 254

Hi, my name is Candice. I won *The Great British Bake Off* in 2016. I run a successful pub with my brother, I have written a book (this is my second), and I write recipes for various publications. I travel far and wide on my own and regularly go on stage to demonstrate cookery in front of huge crowds. I have appeared on TV numerous times.

I also have depression, PTSD (Post-traumatic stress disorder) and chronic phobia. Oh, and this year I was diagnosed with ADHD (Attention deficit hyperactivity disorder), which explains a lot!!

When I write this down it looks like two different people introducing themselves to you, but I am both.

Mental health is something that is becoming more and more frequently talked about in society; it is becoming more recognised, and less stigmatised. I will never claim to be an expert or give advice but what I do know is what has helped me, what has got me through some of my darkest days and what has kept me going... and that is food. Food and cooking.

For me, food has always been about more than just eating. It is the cooking, the process from start to finish that I love. From the first thought or idea that excites you, gets your senses going and your mouth watering, to choosing each ingredient and turning them into something tasty, comforting and exciting. Even when it doesn't go to plan, cooking raises my spirits. It still usually tastes good even if it's not what I planned!

I've often spoken about cooking being my thing – the only thing I've ever felt comes naturally. Because of this, I cook not only because I want to, but because I need to. Cooking is a saviour for me. Learning from mistakes and knowing what to do to improve it next time – this process is how I learn to be a better cook and is also my kind of therapy.

Cooking gives me confidence when I feel my least confident. It reminds me I can do something good, that I can make people smile and bring joy through something I have done myself. Cooking reminds me that I am good enough.

The kitchen has always been my happy place. My first memories of my Nan are in the kitchen, me stood next to her watching her making pastry, Yorkshire puddings and my grandad's favourite cakes. The kitchen is the place I always gravitate to, whether it's at a family gathering, friends' houses, parties or visiting restaurants – I'll always ask for a little look or try to linger there. It's the only place I feel completely at ease.

I cook and bake when I'm happy, when I'm sad, when I'm bored, anxious or fidgety – which I now know is sometimes down to my ADHD – when that dark cloud surrounds me like a thick, heavy burden and I have no idea why. It's my place. Cooking has got me through some proper shit times, and it continues to do so.

Our lives are busy, sometimes chaotic and often unexpected things happen. Well, that's how I might describe mine anyway. Things change, don't go to plan, derail us, upset us, shock us and that's OK. What we need to do, sometimes, is just slow down, take time and take stock of the things that we enjoy and that make us happy – or at least smile for a while.

My mental health is something I hadn't really spoken about until fairly recently, but it is something I've been battling with for quite a few years. I have had days where I didn't want to get out of bed, I've cancelled plans, not spoken to family and friends and felt completely useless. But I have also accomplished things I never thought possible – and probably other people never thought possible – and that is because I found something I love. Cooking at home puts me in my comfort zone and cooking outside my kitchen pushes me out of my comfort zone too, which is a good thing.

If you are like me – and I have recently found out so many of you are – you take to your kitchen to sooth anxieties, calm yourself and make yourself smile. Cooking has brought a whole load of us together through that mutual love. That and long hot baths, cake and chicken nuggets!

This book contains recipes that I want to share with you so I can spread some of the joy they give me (a bath is optional!). These recipes are simple to follow, easy to adapt if you are missing an ingredient and perfectly delicious. Many of them are quick to make because life is busy. It should be no surprise that some of my favourite bakes and cakes feature here, celebrating the simple British pleasure and comfort you get from having a cup of tea and a slice of cake or a gooey warm cookie – or both! These small moments of joy just seem to make life a little bit better. Even more so, if shared.

Throughout this book you will find lots of simple, comforting meals because I find that one of the tricky things to do when life gets a little bit tough is to find meal inspiration. These are some of my favourite recipes and things to eat that have got me through low times and frazzled weeks, when my feet don't touch the ground and my brain feels like mush. These old friends from my kitchen have methodical, tried-and-tested, familiar steps that never fail to take my mind off worries and offer delicious pick-me-up flavours that feel like a hug for my taste buds. They put a smile on my face and raise my spirits, so I can get that lipstick on, ready to face another day.

I have tried to keep everything simple yet hearty and easy to adapt to the seasons and what you might have in the cupboard and fridge. This is food that fills your belly and lifts your spirits. There are recipes here that you can make in one pan – throw a load of ingredients together, whack in the oven and return to after you've hidden under the duvet for a little while. Even better, you'll have leftovers for another day or the base for a second meal.

There are other recipes that will help you while away a weekend's worries, keeping those fidgety hands and your overworked brain busy. These are my self-care recipes – lots of calming processes, such as making bread, shaping pastry for a pie, or decorating extravagant celebration cakes that you can share with your loved ones, to offer as a gift or have a big ol' slice yourself while watching your favourite film!

We can often forget number one and get easily overwhelmed. We need to ensure we take time for ourselves and be kind to, not only everyone else, but ourselves too. I hope this book will help you do that.

This book doesn't aim for perfect. It aims for deliciousness.

You won't find any guilty food chats, no rules and no judgement. Just good, simple nourishment from proper food made with love and care.

Happy cooking!
Candice x

Quick pick-me-ups

SAVOURY:

Fancy eggs – 14

Cauliflower, coconut and corn fritters – 16

Tortilla-crusted halloumi chips – 17

Parmesan-crusted courgette and asparagus with tzatziki – 21

Prawn and chorizo fried rice – 22

The ultimate toastie – 25

Spinach, mushroom and blue cheese pancakes – 26

Herb and oat salmon fish fingers with tartare mayo – 29

SWEET:

Croissant french toast – 30

Chocolate, orange and stem ginger shortbread – 31

Oozy gooey double chocolate one-pan cookies – 32

Apple and blackberry fool – 36

Cinnamon pastry twists with chocolate sauce – 39

Truffles – 40

Coconut and lime scones – 41

Whack-it-all-in chocolate cornflake rocky road – 42

Hot chocolate orange – 45

Baileys and banana chocolate milkshake – 46

WHEN I AM feeling particularly low, I start picking at things in the kitchen, raiding the cupboard and gravitating towards food like crisps, cheese and chicken nuggets – things that are instantly available and settle cravings – if only briefly.

For those days when you just don't fancy going out, don't really want to speak to people, can't face going to the shops and don't want to spend hours making something to eat, it's important to keep yourself nourished and fed. Eating ice cream out of the tub can only curb a certain amount of food cravings and Creme Eggs only provide limited nutrition!

So, the recipes in this chapter offer a bit more sustenance, but with minimal effort. Hopefully giving you a full and satisfied feeling that lasts a bit longer than eating a bag of crisps or a box of chocolates. I'm not saying never eat crisps or sweet treats, and there are even some of my own versions of my favourite snacks in here.

If you fancy something sweet, but making a full-on cake is out of the question and your patience for anything else is pretty thin, these quick-and-easy home-cooked meals and treats will put a smile on your face and fill your belly. They can all be ready in 30 minutes or less and you can easily swap ingredients for whatever you have in your fridge or cupboard. Easy to double, triple or quadruple, you can make these for yourself and family and friends too.

Fancy eggs

SERVES 2

olive oil
1 yellow pepper, deseeded
 and diced
6 spring onions, finely sliced
½ courgette, sliced
6 mushrooms, sliced (I used
 chestnut mushrooms)
1 garlic clove, finely chopped
1 red chilli, sliced, or ½ tsp
 chilli flakes
knob of butter
200g 'nduja, torn, or chorizo
 or salami, skin removed and
 roughly chopped into discs
100g baby spinach
4 eggs
20g Parmesan cheese
salt and freshly ground
 black pepper

The quickest recipe you can make and it's a proper good one for using up all the odds and sods in the fridge. 'Nduja – can I say this word? No, I can't, but it's sooooo tasty! You can get this in most supermarkets, but chorizo, ham hock or even sausage is fab, too. Veggie? Then leave it out. Eggs are normally thought of for breakfast, but I say no to that – eggs are for all day! Spicy, not spicy, runny or firm – you do your eggs *your* way, but make them fancy.

Place a non-stick frying pan over a medium-high heat and add a glug of olive oil.

Add the pepper, spring onions, courgette and mushrooms and fry until they start to soften and take on colour. Add the garlic, chilli or chilli flakes and butter. Stir. Add the 'nduja or chopped sausage of your choice and break it up with a wooden spoon, stirring and cooking as you go. Add the spinach and stir until wilted – about 1 minute.

Make a well in the middle of the vegetables and nduja and crack in the eggs. Season with salt and pepper and allow to cook for a couple of seconds. You can either leave these as they are, like fried eggs nestled in the mixture, or mix the eggs vigorously trying to keep the now scrambled egg in the middle of the pan. Just as the egg starts to cook, remove the pan from the heat.

Divide the eggs between two plates and serve scattered with a grating of the Parmesan.

Cauliflower, coconut + corn fritters

SERVES 4

about 300g cauliflower
100g plain flour
½ tsp baking powder
½ tsp cumin seeds
½ tsp smoked paprika
½ tsp chilli flakes
1 egg
140ml whole milk
200g sweetcorn (I used
    frozen and defrosted)
25g desiccated coconut
2 spring onions, finely
    chopped
150g Gouda cheese
knob of coconut oil
salt and freshly ground
    black pepper
Tzatziki (page 21) or
    tomato and avocado
    salsa, to serve

I think sweetcorn gets massively overlooked and is either put on a plate as an afterthought – mixed in with peas (just no) or as corn on the cob. This recipe makes it the star of the show. Cauliflower is one of my favourite vegetables so bringing these ingredients together means flavour, texture and a lovely little plate of food. Of course, I've got spice in there – I don't know why a little bit of chilli seems to make me happy, maybe it's the heat.

Roughly chop the cauliflower into varying sized pieces and remove any big bits of stalk. You can use the leaves too.

Bring a saucepan of salted water to the boil, then drop in the cauliflower and boil for 4 minutes. Drop the leaves in with about 1 minute to go. Drain, shake and leave to dry out on a clean tea towel or kitchen towel.

Put the flour, baking powder, cumin seeds, paprika, chilli flakes and some salt and pepper in a large bowl and mix together. Create a well in the middle and crack in the egg. Whisk, bringing the flour in from the edges until you have a thick batter.

Add a stream of milk as you whisk and continue to whisk until the batter is smooth and lump free. Add the sweetcorn, coconut, spring onions and cooled cauliflower, stir through, then grate in the Gouda and mix together.

Heat a large frying pan over a medium-high heat and add the coconut oil. Once melted, add a small bit of batter and fry until cooked, then taste for seasoning. Adjust the seasoning as necessary.

Add 1 tablespoon of batter to the hot pan – you should be able to cook about four fritters at a time (you can make them bigger or smaller). Fry on one side for 1–2 minutes until bubbles appear on the uncooked side, then flip over and fry until golden. Keep warm in the oven and continue to fry in batches until you have used all the batter.

Serve with tzatziki or tomato and avocado salsa. You can freeze these cooked for up to one month. Just defrost and warm in the oven.

Tortilla-crusted halloumi chips

SERVES 2

50g tortilla chips (I used
   cheese flavour)
½ tsp dried oregano
pinch of freshly ground
   black pepper
25g Parmesan cheese,
   grated (optional)
½ tsp paprika (optional)
225g halloumi
olive oil
mixed salad and tomato
   salsa, to serve

This recipe came about as I didn't have any polenta to crust my halloumi with, but I did have half a bag of cheese flavour tortilla chips. I bashed them up, added more cheese and some herbs and bingo – the ultimate squeaky cheese feast. Soph, you know this is for you! You can use any flavour of tortilla chips or crisps, or even the more traditional polenta if you fancy.

Blitz the tortilla chips in a food processor or blender until they form coarse crumbs. (You can also do this the old-fashioned way by putting them in a bag and bashing with a rolling pin!) Add the oregano and pepper and mix through. If you're using plain tortilla chips or want an extra flavour boost, add the grated Parmesan and paprika too.

Slice the halloumi into fat, chip-style pieces and coat in the olive oil. Tip the tortilla crumbs on to a plate and roll the halloumi pieces in them until they are completely covered in the crumbs.

Heat a glug of olive oil in a frying pan over a medium-high heat and add the halloumi chips. Fry for about 2 minutes until they are golden brown and have started to soften, then flip over and fry for a further 1–2 minutes.

Serve on a bed of mixed salad with tomato salsa to dip.

Parmesan-crusted courgette + asparagus with tzatziki

SERVES 2-4

350g plain flour
1 tsp dried oregano
75g Grana Padano
  cheese, finely grated
½ tsp garlic salt
large pinch of freshly
  ground black pepper
700ml soda water
2 courgettes
300g asparagus
olive oil
sea salt flakes

TZATZIKI:
250g Greek yoghurt
½ cucumber, grated and
  juice squeezed out
small bunch of fresh dill,
  chopped
zest of 1 lemon, plus juice
  of ½
1 garlic clove, crushed
drizzle of olive oil
sprinkle of paprika

One of my favourite things to eat in Greece is fried courgettes dipped in fresh tzatziki. I love that you can now get them as courgette fries here too and always order them if they're on the menu. These are so easy to make – crunchy, yummy and perfect as a sharer. You can use most vegetables, but make sure they are sliced thinly enough that they can cook through. You should have some tzatziki left over to pop in a sandwich too.

Put the flour, oregano, Grana Padano, garlic salt and pepper in a bowl and mix together. Create a well in the middle of the dry ingredients and slowly pour the soda water into the well, whisking constantly until you have a smooth thin batter.

Cut the top and bottom off the courgettes, then cut them in half and slice lengthways into thin strips (about 3mm).

If the asparagus is untrimmed, bend the ends until they snap and throw away the woody end bits of stalk (that's the tough bit!).

Heat a good glug of olive oil in a large frying pan over a medium heat – enough so that it almost covers the bottom of the pan.

Dip the courgette strips and asparagus spears into the batter and transfer to the hot pan in batches. Fry for 1–2 minutes on each side until golden brown and crispy. Remove from the pan and keep warm in the oven while you fry the rest.

To make the tzatziki, add all the ingredients except the olive oil and paprika to a bowl and mix together. Transfer to a serving dish or bowl, drizzle over the olive oil, then sprinkle with the paprika.

Serve the hot courgettes and asparagus sprinkled with sea salt flakes and the tzatziki for dipping.

Prawn + chorizo fried rice

SERVES 2

glug of sesame or olive oil

60g chorizo, skin removed, cut in half lengthways and sliced

1 red onion, finely chopped

6 baby corn, each chopped into 4 pieces

6 mushrooms, sliced (oyster mushrooms are great for this dish but chestnut are fine)

handful of broccoli florets

1 red, green, yellow or orange pepper, deseeded and sliced

1 red chilli, finely chopped, or 1 tsp chilli paste

2 garlic cloves, finely chopped

150g raw king prawns

1 x 250g packet ready-cooked wholegrain rice (or cooked rice of your choice)

splash of chilli oil (optional)

1 egg

splash of light soy sauce

25g salted cashews, roughly chopped

I'm not joking when I say I have this dish at least three or four times a week. I like loads of spice, so I add lots of chilli along with the chorizo and garlic – vampires beware! My little trick with the egg at the end means you don't get scrambled eggs or weird eggy strips, but it soaks up the flavours and coats the rice. You might think it's a cop out using microwavable rice, but it's perfect for when you don't have the time or energy to cook rice.

Heat a wok or large frying pan over a medium heat, add a glug of oil and the chorizo and move the chorizo around for a minute to release some of its oil. Add the onion, baby corn, mushrooms, broccoli, pepper and chilli and fry for 5–6 minutes until the veg starts to soften and turn golden brown.

Add the garlic and prawns and cook until the prawns start to turn from grey to pink – this takes literally 2 minutes. Add the rice and keep moving and frying for a further 2 minutes until piping hot.

Working fast, create a hole in the middle of the prawn and veg mix, increase the heat, add a splash of chilli oil, if using, then crack in the egg. Add a splash of soy sauce on to the egg, then wait a few seconds as the egg starts to set and beat it together so it starts to scramble. Mix through the prawns, veg and rice.

Scatter with chopped cashews and serve immediately.

This recipe is great with noodles too, or on top of a baked sweet potato.

The ultimate toastie

MAKES 1

2 thick slices of bread of
  your choice
1 tsp mayonnaise
1 egg
2 cooked veggie or meat
  sausages, halved lengthways
¼ red onion, finely sliced
2 slices of cheese (I used
  Emmental)
salt and freshly ground
  black pepper

You might think there is no place for the humble toastie in a cookbook, but let me tell you, this is where you're wrong. The toastie has come a long way recently and this guy has it all and more. Cheese, of course, plus sausage, onions and, if you get it right, a runny egg. Or if you are a bit weird like me, pick out the hard yolk and give it to your mam! You can literally put anything in a toastie, even peanut butter and cheese works.

Preheat a sandwich toaster or place a frying pan over a medium heat.

Spread half the mayonnaise over one slice of bread. Turn the bread over and, using your fingers, push down the middle of the bread to create a slight bowl shape. Crack the egg into the bread bowl – it's up to you if you want to break the yolk – and season with salt and pepper. Top with the cooked sausages, onion and finally the cheese. Put the second slice of bread on top and spread the remaining mayonnaise over the outside of the bread.

Carefully lift the sandwich into the sandwich toaster or frying pan. To cook in the sandwich toaster, close the lid and cook it's until golden brown, the cheese is oozing, and the egg is cooked. In a frying pan, cook for 3–4 minutes on each side and flip carefully. You may need to finish it off in the oven. If so, simply place it on a baking tray and cook for about 5 minutes at 160°C fan (180°C/350°F/Gas Mark 4).

Remove from the heat and slice in half – be very careful as the filling will be piping hot.

Simple toastie

2 thick slices of bread
1 tbsp crunchy peanut butter
3 rashers of streaky bacon,
  cooked
2 slices of Cheddar cheese
1 tsp mayonnaise

Spread the peanut butter over one slice of bread, then add the cooked bacon and top with the cheese. Put the second slice of bread on top and spread over half the mayonnaise. Flip on to a sandwich toaster so it is mayonnaise-side down. Spread the remaining mayonnaise over the upturned slice of bread. Close the lid and cook until toasted, golden and oozing. Please mind your mouth... it's hottttttttt!

Spinach, mushroom + blue cheese pancakes

**SERVES 2 AS A MAIN
OR 4 AS A LIGHT MEAL**

PANCAKE BATTER:
60g plain flour
60g buckwheat flour
2 eggs
300ml whole milk
small bunch of fresh chives,
    finely chopped
30g unsalted butter, melted
salt and freshly ground
    black pepper

FILLING:
glug of olive oil
knob of butter
250g mixed mushrooms, sliced
    (chestnut, small portobello
    and button work well)
½ onion, finely chopped
1 garlic clove, finely chopped
200g baby spinach
150g Gorgonzola cheese
30g pine nuts
25g Parmesan cheese, grated

I eat pancakes a lot and always choose savoury over sweet. They are so versatile and can be filled with pretty much anything you have in your fridge, but cheese, oozing and stretching as you take a bite always wins for me. Can't be arsed to make pancakes? Then whack this on toast for an even quicker pick-me-up. Perfect fast and filling food.

Preheat the grill to medium-high.

To make the batter for the pancakes, add both flours to a large bowl with a good pinch of salt and pepper. Make a well in the centre and crack in the eggs. Mix together using a whisk. Add the milk and chives and mix in, whisking energetically to remove any lumps. Whisk in 2 tablespoons of the melted butter and leave to sit for about 15 minutes while you get on with the filling.

Set a large frying pan over a medium-high heat and add the olive oil and butter. Drop in the mushrooms and onion, stir and cook for 4–5 minutes until they start to colour.

Stir in the garlic and keep frying for 2–3 minutes until everything is slightly golden and cooked. Add the spinach and move about until wilted, then remove from the heat. Drop in the Gorgonzola and stir until melted together. Season to taste. Set aside.

Wash out the frying pan, dry and set over a medium heat. Dip a piece of kitchen paper into the remaining melted butter and wipe around the pan. Add a ladleful of the batter and swirl to cover the base of the pan. Fry for about 2 minutes until bubbles start to form and the edges of the pancake lift. Flip over and cook the other side until golden. Slide the cooked pancake on to a baking tray and fry the next pancake. While you are doing this, add a good helping of the mushroom mix on to one half of the cooked pancake. Fold that in half, then into quarters. Repeat with the next cooked pancake and then the rest of the batter and mushroom mix, placing the filled pancakes on to the tray so that they are slightly overlapping each other.

Sprinkle over the pine nuts and Parmesan, then place under the grill until the Parmesan is melted and bubbling, the pancakes are crispy, and the pine nuts are golden. Serve hot and gooey.

Herb + oat salmon fish fingers with tartare mayo

SERVES 2-3

50g rolled oats
25g Parmesan cheese, grated
small bunch of fresh curly
 parsley
zest of 1 lemon
1 garlic clove
2 salmon fillets (or fish of
 your choice)
salt and freshly ground
 black pepper
bap, Little Gem lettuce leaves
 and sliced cucumber, to
 serve (optional)

TARTARE MAYONNAISE:

2 tbsp mayonnaise
2 large gherkins or 6
 cornichons, finely chopped
1 tsp capers or 2 spring onions,
 finely chopped
squeeze of lemon juice
small bunch of fresh chives,
 finely chopped

A fish finger sandwich is one of my favourite things to eat and I really go to town on them sometimes – cheese, bacon, lettuce, tartare, beans to dip in... You get the gist. But these homemade fish fingers are a bit posh and very tasty. I love the subtle herbs and the crunch from the oats. You can use any fish you like – the thickness may alter the cooking time, but not too much. They work great in a sarnie, but also with chips and beans for a comfort-food-style school dinner!

Preheat the oven to 160°C fan (180°C/350°F/Gas Mark 4).

Put the oats, Parmesan, parsley, lemon zest, garlic and some salt and pepper in a food processor or small blender. Blitz until you have a medium crumbs and all the ingredients are combined.

Using a sharp knife, slice each salmon fillet into 4–5 finger-sized pieces.

Tip the herb and oat crumbs on to a plate and toss the fish pieces in the crumbs, pushing the crumbs on so they stick to the fish. Place the fish fingers on a baking tray and bake for 10–12 minutes until cooked through. Slightly bigger pieces may need a bit longer.

Meanwhile, put all the ingredients for the tartare mayo in a bowl and mix well. Set aside.

Serve the fish fingers with a big dollop of the tartare mayonnaise. Alternatively, enjoy in a fresh bap with Little Gem lettuce, cucumber and the tartare mayo for the ultimate fish finger sandwich.

Croissant french toast

SERVES 2

2 eggs
100ml whole milk
½ tsp ground cinnamon
2 plain croissants (big or
    small – it's up to you)
knob of butter

TOPPINGS:
6 rashers of smoked
    streaky bacon
25g pecans
maple syrup

OR:
6 rashers of smoked streaky
    bacon, chopped
100g mushrooms, sliced
    (I used chestnut)
1 red chilli, chopped
about 100g baby spinach
dollop of ricotta cheese
salt and freshly ground
    black pepper

If you are going to have French toast, then let's make it proper French toast and get those croissants soaking up all that egg. I have eaten this late at night, feeling crappy and it has instantly put a smile on my face. I love the sweetness from the croissants against the smoky bacon and mushrooms and then there's also the option of bacon, maple syrup and pecans. It can also be simplified and eaten with no toppings at all and really is just as good.

Beat the eggs, milk and cinnamon together in a bowl. Slice the croissants in half lengthways and dip into the egg mixture. Turn and leave to soak for 5 minutes.

Put a large frying pan over a medium heat, add the butter and swirl until melted. Add the eggy croissant halves and fry for 2–3 minutes on each side until golden brown and the egg is cooked. You can either keep them warm in a warm oven or in a separate pan while cooking the topping.

For a sweet topping, add the streaky bacon to a frying pan over a medium heat and cook until crispy. About halfway through cooking, throw in the pecans and toast in the bacon fat.

Layer the bacon and pecans on the warm eggy croissants and drizzle over some maple syrup. Serve hot.

For a savoury topping, add the bacon, mushrooms and chilli to a frying pan over a medium-high heat and fry until the bacon is cooked and the mushrooms are golden brown. Add the spinach and stir until wilted and hot. Season with salt and pepper to taste.

Tip on to the eggy croissants, top with the ricotta and season with salt and pepper. Serve hot.

Chocolate, orange + stem ginger shortbread

MAKES ABOUT 25–30 DEPENDING ON THE SIZE OF CUTTER

85g golden caster sugar
zest of 1 orange
170g unsalted butter, softened
245g plain flour, plus extra for dusting
pinch of salt
75g crystallised stem ginger, chopped
100g dark chocolate (minimum 70% cocoa solids)
sea salt flakes

Shortbread was one of the first things I learned to bake on my own and I imagine it's the same for a lot of people, whether it was at home or in food technology at school. It is so, so easy to make and you can add any flavours (dried fruit works best as fresh gives off too much juice), make it any shape and it's great to bake with children or package up as little gifts. If it makes it out of the kitchen, of course.

Put the sugar and orange zest in a bowl and mash the zest into the sugar with the back of a spoon so the oils get into the sugar and you can smell the orange. Add the softened butter and mix until combined. Add the flour and salt and start to mix with a wooden spoon then start to work with your hands. Add the stem ginger and mix until combined – do not over work the dough or you have tough shortbread.

Remove the dough from the bowl, flatten and wrap in clingfilm. Transfer to the fridge to chill for 10 minutes.

Preheat the oven to 160°C fan (180°C/350°F/Gas Mark 4) and line a baking tray with greaseproof paper.

Lightly flour a work surface and roll the dough into a 1cm-thick rectangle. Cut in half lengthways, then into smaller rectangles – like fingers. Place the biscuits on to the prepared tray with space in between each one and put in the freezer for 5 minutes.

Bake for 12–15 minutes until golden brown, then leave to cool on a wire rack.

Melt the chocolate either in a microwavable bowl in 20-second bursts in the microwave or in a heatproof bowl set over a saucepan of simmering water.

Dip each shortbread finger into the melted chocolate up to halfway. Place back on a piece of greaseproof paper and sprinkle with a few sea salt flakes. Leave to set.

The shortbread will keep for up to three days in an airtight biscuit tin.

Oozy gooey double chocolate one-pan cookies

**MAKES 1 LARGE COOKIE
OR LOTS OF LITTLE ONES**

250g unsalted butter, softened,
   plus extra for greasing
250g golden caster sugar
100g light soft brown sugar
3 eggs
2 tsp vanilla bean paste
375g plain flour
2 tsp baking powder
½ tsp salt
150g white chocolate chips or
   white chocolate, chopped
150g dark chocolate chips or
   dark chocolate (minimum
   70% cocoa solids), chopped
150g pistachios, roughly
   chopped
pinch of sea salt flakes

Need a soft-in-the-middle cookie quick sharp? Look no further. This went down an absolute treat as a pudding in the pub served with a big scoop of ice cream on top. Do not, I repeat do not, overcook it. You want it barely cooked in the middle so it's gooey, runny and sexy. You can add nuts, dried fruit or peanut butter should you wish. Make a big one or little individual ones – you choose. The dough freezes well too, so you can have your cookie and eat it… any time you need a really quick sweet treat or sugar fix or when Matt comes to stay!

Preheat the oven to 160°C fan (180°C/350°F/Gas Mark 4) and grease an ovenproof mini frying pan with some butter.

Mix the butter and both sugars together in a large bowl until light and whipped, using either serious elbow grease and a wooden spoon, a handheld electric mixer or a free-standing electric mixer. This will take a couple of minutes. Add the eggs and vanilla bean paste and mix well until combined. If it starts to curdle, add a little flour. Add the (remaining) flour, baking powder and salt and mix to combine. Fold through both types of chocolate and the pistachios.

For a 13cm frying pan, place about 2 tablespoons of the cookie dough into the pan. You will need slightly less for smaller pans and slightly more for bigger pans. You can also make one large cookie, but this will increase the cooking time significantly.

OPTIONAL EXTRAS:
crunchy peanut butter
chocolate spread
speculoos biscuit spread
jam
caramel
chocolate cookies with
    cream filling

If you'd like to add one of the optional extras, add 1 teaspoon of the spread of your choice (peanut butter, jam, caramel etc) to the middle of the cookie dough before baking or put a cookie underneath the dough.

Bake in the oven for 5–7 minutes for super gooey individual cookies. Cook the large cookie for 25–35 minutes. The middle should be super soft and wobbly.

Remove from the oven and leave to stand for a minute before plopping on a scoop of vanilla ice cream. Serve hot in the pan.

The cookie dough will last for up to 4 days wrapped in the fridge or up to a month in the freezer. Simply slice off a chunk when you want a freshly baked cookie.

Apple + blackberry fool

MAKES 4–6 INDIVIDUAL FOOLS

100g blackberries
juice of 1 lemon
½ tsp ground cinnamon
4 tbsp icing sugar
200g apples, peeled, cored
  and grated (I used Braeburn)
500ml double cream

TO FINISH:
blackberries
dried apple slices (see below)
sprig of fresh mint
chopped hazelnuts

Who are you calling a fool? Fools can often be summery, but I've given this a little autumn twist. It's even better if you can pick your own fruit. You can serve these in cute little glasses or just dive in to one with a big spoon. Mix it up with whatever flavours you like, but try to get a little tartness in there to balance out the sweetness.

Blitz the blackberries in a food processor or in a bowl with a handheld electric mixer. Squeeze the lemon juice over the berries and sprinkle over the cinnamon and icing sugar. Blitz lightly – you still want lumps and bits of fruit, not a purée. Mix through the grated apple and leave to stand for 10 minutes.

Whip the double cream until smooth soft peaks form. Fold through 5–6 tablespoons of the apple and blackberry mixture so you have a marbled effect.

Place some of the apple and blackberry mixture in the bottom of 4–6 serving glasses and then add some of the cream mixture, then a little more fruit mixture, then more cream and finish with a drizzle of fruit mixture. Top with a fresh blackberry, a dried apple slice, a sprig of mint and a sprinkle of hazelnuts. Serve immediately or place in the fridge until needed – you can prepare these a good couple hours ahead of time if you need to.

Dried apple slices

Slice an apple into very thin rounds with the core through the middle. Place on a baking tray lined with greaseproof paper and dry in a very low oven at 100°C fan (120°C/250°F/Gas Mark ½) for several hours or overnight until completely dried out. These will keep for a couple of weeks in an airtight container if completely dry.

Cinnamon pastry twists with chocolate sauce

MAKES A SHARING BOWL FULL

200g piece of puff pastry or cut-offs of puff pastry
100g caster sugar
1 tsp ground cinnamon
½ tsp ground ginger

CHOCOLATE SAUCE:
200ml double cream
1 tbsp golden syrup
150g dark chocolate (minimum 70% cocoa solids), chopped
40g unsalted butter

This idea came from having pastry cut-offs left over from making pies and not wanting to throw them away, so I twisted them, stuck them on a baking tray, then tossed them in cinnamon sugar and popped them on the bar for a sweet bar snack. If you're going to have a pastry twist, then you've got to have a little dip too! Quite simply the easiest little treat you'll make. If you want to go that extra mile, you can make your own puff pastry from scratch.

Preheat the oven to 180°C fan (200°C/400°F/Gas Mark 6) and line a baking tray with greaseproof paper.

Cut the puff pastry sheet into 1cm strips about 10–13cm long. Twist the puff pastry strips and gently place on the baking tray, pushing the ends down to secure the twist. If using cut-offs, the twists may be slightly different shapes and sizes but that's OK! Bake for 10–15 minutes until golden brown and crisp.

Mix the sugar, cinnamon and ginger together in a bowl. Toss the warm pastry twists in the spiced sugar until evenly coated and then place in separate bowl.

To make the chocolate sauce, pour the cream and golden syrup into a saucepan and simmer until bubbling around the edges. Remove from the heat and add the chocolate. Leave to stand for 5 minutes, before stirring vigorously until smooth. Add the butter and mix until glossy.

Serve the chocolate sauce alongside the cinnamon pastry twists and dip until your heart's content! Definitely best eaten warm out the oven.

Truffles

MAKES PLENTY TO EAT YOURSELF, WRAP AND SHARE

250ml double cream
50g unsalted butter
250g good-quality dark chocolate chips or dark chocolate (minimum 70% cocoa solids, but the higher the better), chopped

COFFEE & HAZELNUT:
50ml Tia Maria
50g hazelnuts, chopped

MINT CHOCOLATE & COCONUT:
½ tsp peppermint extract
25g desiccated coconut

CHOCOLATE ORANGE:
zest of 1 orange
50ml Grand Marnier
20g cocoa powder

I don't think I could hide my shock when I realised how to make truffles. Literally just two ingredients should you wish! The beauty with these is that you can add different flavours to them, roll them in different ingredients to make them look pretty and when you tell people you made your own truffles they will think you are a chocolate genius. The perfect bite-sized pick-me-up.

Put the cream and butter in a saucepan over a medium heat and heat until bubbles start to break all over the surface. Remove from the heat and tip in the chocolate. Set aside for 5 minutes, then stir to mix through until smooth and glossy.

Divide the melted chocolate into three bowls. Add the Tia Maria to one bowl, the peppermint extract to the second and mix the orange zest and Grand Marnier through the third. Place all the bowls into the fridge until the chocolate is set and mouldable.

Line a baking tray with greaseproof paper.

Place the chopped hazelnuts on a plate, the coconut on a second plate and the cocoa powder on a third. Using a teaspoon, scoop out the thickened chocolate mixture and roll into balls about half the size of a golf ball. I find this easiest wearing gloves. Roll the Tia-Maria-flavoured chocolate in the chopped hazelnuts, the peppermint-flavoured chocolate in the coconut and the chocolate orange in the cocoa. Set out on the lined baking tray and return to the fridge to set completely.

Serve after dinner, give as a gift or just eat yourself as a lovely luxury treat!

These keep for about five days in the fridge, remove 10 minutes before eating.

Coconut + lime scones

MAKES 6-8

300g self-raising flour,
 plus extra for dusting
150g strong white bread flour
2 tsp baking powder
pinch of salt
75g coconut oil
50g golden caster sugar
25g desiccated coconut
zest of 2 limes
about 200ml whole milk
2 eggs
clotted cream and raspberry
 jam, to serve

Scones with coconut oil, yes they work. Use a really good coconut oil and you get a beautiful flavour as well as a lovely fluffy texture. I love anything coconut flavoured so these are perfect. Again, speedy to make, but a really lovely combination and served warm with a dollop of coconut cream they are even better. No cutters, no problem – go off-piste and cut them into squares.

Preheat the oven to 200°C fan (220°C/425°F/Gas Mark 7) and line a large, flat baking tray with greaseproof paper.

Put the flours, baking powder and a pinch of salt in a large bowl. Add the coconut oil and rub in with your fingertips until the mixture resembles breadcrumbs. Stir in the sugar, desiccated coconut and lime zest.

Pour the milk into a jug. Add the eggs and mix together – it should make up to about 275ml.

Make a well in middle of the flour mixture. Pour in three quarters of the egg-milk mixture and use a blunt knife to mix together. Add more if it's looking a little dry (save a little to glaze). Finish mixing with your hands, but be careful not to handle the dough too much.

Lightly flour a clean work surface. Turn out the dough and use your hands to knead it lightly, bringing it together. Flatten it to about 5cm thick and cut out the scones with a round 7.5cm cutter. Bring the cuttings back together and continue to cut out until you have used up all the dough.

Place the scones on the prepared tray, making sure you have space in between each one. Brush a little of the leftover milk mixture over each scone, then bake for 12–15 minutes until golden, risen and smelling of coconut.

Serve warm with clotted cream and raspberry jam. Which way round is up to you...!

Best eaten on the day they are made but they can be rewarmed in the oven with a little splash of water the next day.

Whack-it-all-in chocolate cornflake rocky road

**MAKES ABOUT
9 SQUARES**

250g dark chocolate
   (70% cocoa solids for a more
   grown-up flavour), chopped
   or dark chocolate chips
125g unsalted butter, cubed
4 tbsp golden syrup
100g cornflakes
100g oaty biscuits
75g dried cherries
50g sultanas
100g marshmallows either
   mini or larger ones roughly
   chopped
50g pecans
100g chocolate caramel bars
50g white chocolate, chopped
   or white chocolate chips

The title basically says it all. Any leftover chocolate (though when I have chocolate left over I don't know), old Easter eggs or odd biscuits, then whack it all in, melt it together and pop it in the fridge. The nice thing about this recipe is that you can theme it for different times of the year – bunnies and chicks for Easter, snowflakes and reindeer for Christmas. Other cereal works well too.

Heat a saucepan of water over a medium heat until simmering. Place a heatproof bowl over the saucepan, but don't let the water touch the bottom of the bowl (this is a bain-marie). Put the dark chocolate, butter and golden syrup in the bowl and melt slowly, stirring with a wooden spoon. Once melted, remove from the heat and leave to cool slightly.

Stir through the cornflakes. Break up the oaty biscuits, then add them to the melted chocolate along with the remaining ingredients, except the chocolate caramel bars and white chocolate. Gently fold through so everything is evenly coated in melted chocolate.

Line a 20 x 20cm baking dish with greaseproof paper and scrape the mixture evenly into the tray. Gently spread it out but leave it jagged and lumpy.

Break or cut up the chocolate caramel bars and dot over the top.

Melt the white chocolate in a bain-marie or in 20-second bursts in a microwave. Drizzle the melted chocolate over the top of the rocky road, then transfer to the fridge to set for 20–30 minutes for a soft-set rocky road.

Any leftovers will keep in an airtight container in the fridge or a cool place for up to one week.

Hot chocolate orange

MAKES 2

600ml whole milk (whole milk
   works best, but you can use
   alternatives such as coconut,
   soy or oat milk)
zest of 1 orange
1 cardamom pod
50g dark chocolate chips or
   dark chocolate (minimum
   70% cocoa solids), chopped
2 tsp light soft brown sugar
50ml Cointreau (optional)
100ml double cream
pinch of ground cinnamon
dried orange slices (optional)

**Winter. Open fire. Slice of cake. Hot chocolate with orange.
Check. Get your bobble hat on and pull up a comfy seat. This is
indulgent, sweet, chocolatey and slightly spicy and the Cointreau
makes it really grown up. Leave out the Cointreau for the kids,
or if you're teetotal, and it's still lovely and comforting without.**

Put the milk, orange zest and cardamom pod in a saucepan and
set over a low-medium heat until gently simmering with bubbles
breaking the surface. Remove from the heat and add the chocolate,
then leave to stand without stirring for a minute. Stir really well until
all the chocolate has melted.

Add 1 teaspoon of brown sugar and 25ml Cointreau, if using,
to two mugs, cups or fancy heatproof glasses. Pour over the hot
chocolate mixture, removing the cardamom pod. Stir until the
sugar has dissolved.

Whisk the double cream in a small bowl until it's thick enough to
coat the back of a spoon.

Using an upside-down teaspoon, pour the cream on top of the
hot chocolates so it floats on top. Sprinkle over the cinnamon and
garnish with dried orange slices, if you have them.

Baileys + banana chocolate milkshake

MAKES 2

1 banana, peeled
600ml whole milk (coconut
milk tastes great too)
4 large scoops of chocolate
ice cream
100ml Baileys
big handful of ice cubes
chocolate sauce

TO DECORATE:
slice of banana
grated chocolate

I love a milkshake. To be honest, I have a little obsession with anything frozen – ice cream, milkshakes, slushies and ice lollies. This is a drinkable pudding and I am very here for it. There is normally a bottle of Baileys lurking around from Christmas and this recipe is where it came in very handy. A milkshake for the big people among us (leave out the Baileys for the kids though). Add some mint or caramel for an extra treat or try using white chocolate instead of dark.

Put all the ingredients except the chocolate sauce in a blender or smoothie maker and blitz until smooth and thick.

Squirt the chocolate sauce into the bottom and around the inside of two glasses.

Divide the milkshake between the two glasses, top each one with a slice of banana, grate over some chocolate, drop in a paper or reusable straw and get slurping.

Simple comforts

SAVOURY:

Ultimate chicken nuggets – 50

Sweet potato, garlic and red onion tortilla – 53

Lemony tomato, pepper and cod parcels – 54

Chicken sausage, butternut squash and burrata lasagne – 56

Everything-in Bolognese – 60

Goat's cheese, smoked salmon and asparagus filo tart – 62

Pork meatballs with creamy mustard broccoli and orzo – 64

Pesto gnocchi gratin – 67

Spicy chicken and cashew traybake – 68

The best hash browns – kedgeree style! – 72

Arancini (risotto balls) – 74

Charred corn and smoked chilli cornbread – 75

Mushroom, artichoke and tarragon stroganoff – 78

The best potato salad – 79

Crunchy coleslaw – 80

THIS CHAPTER comprises hearty meals that are both easy to make and tasty. Proper comfort food that will fill you up and make you feel better, even if it's just for a little while, because we need to take these moments sometimes – recognise the good feelings and know they are there. Food can do that, so let it. These recipes all taste like a warm hug, which is just what you need after a shitty day. Comfort food has a special place in my heart – my first book was even called *Comfort* – and it's my go-to style of food. I've just simplified it even further for you in this chapter, so you get the best of both worlds.

Here are my throw-it-all-in, super simple meal ideas – perfect for when you don't have the time or energy to cook. They take little effort and require minimum preparation, so result in little mess (though I can't promise this!) and offer maximum taste. As with all my recipes, you can change up the ingredients depending on what you have in the fridge, store cupboard or whatever you might be craving. These dishes are full-on flavour, but super easy, so you have more time to curl up on the sofa with a good book, the dog or cat (or whatever animal you have), your fave series to binge or a familiar happy film and just relax.

Ultimate chicken nuggets

SERVES 4
(I could eat them all
to be honest)

3 skinless chicken breasts
150g cornflakes
50g Parmesan cheese,
   grated
½ tsp garlic powder
small bunch of fresh
   flat-leaf parsley
1 tsp smoked paprika
½ tsp cayenne pepper
1 tsp dried rosemary
salt and freshly ground
   black pepper

**HOMEMADE
BUTTERMILK:**
500ml whole milk
juice of 1 lemon

**SPICY SRIRACHA
MAYO:**
3 tbsp mayonnaise
2 tsp sriracha sauce
   (more if you like it spicy)
zest of 1 lemon
splash of Tabasco sauce
small bunch of fresh chives,
   finely snipped

**Ask anyone what my favourite thing to eat is and they will tell
you chicken nuggets. Good ones, bad ones, takeaway ones and
homemade ones, of course. They are my go-to, especially when I feel
proper shit. I will buy or cook them, add a splodge of mayo and a
sprinkle of salt and work my way through them all. Guilty pleasure?
Nothing guilty about it! Food shouldn't make you feel guilty, just
happy, and chicken nuggets are my ultimate simple comforts.**

Pour the milk and lemon juice into a large bowl and mix together.
Set aside for a couple of minutes and you've got homemade buttermilk!

Chop the chicken into nugget-sized chunks or goujon shapes,
depending on what takes your fancy. Drop the chopped chicken
into the buttermilk, cover with clingfilm and place in the fridge for
at least 3–4 hours or overnight if possible.

Preheat the oven to 160°C fan (180°C/350°F/Gas Mark 4).

Put the cornflakes, grated Parmesan, garlic powder, parsley,
paprika, cayenne pepper, rosemary and some salt and pepper in
a food processor and blitz until rough jagged crumbs form. If you
don't have a food processor, then bash the cornflakes in a Ziplock
bag and finely chop the parsley before mixing all the ingredients
together. Tip in the cornflake mix into a separate bowl.

Remove the chicken from the fridge and roll the marinated nuggets
in the cornflake mix. The cornflakes should stick all over the nuggets,
coating them completely.

Lay the coated nuggets on a baking tray and cook for 18–20
minutes until the nuggets are cooked through and the coating is
crispy and golden.

To make the spicy sriracha mayo, mix all the ingredients together
in a small bowl.

Serve the nuggets hot alongside the spicy mayo – those not feeling
too brave can have plain mayonnaise instead!

Sweet potato, garlic + red onion tortilla

SERVES 4

2 sweet potatoes, peeled
  and thinly sliced
olive oil
2 red onions, finely sliced
1 yellow pepper, deseeded
  and sliced
5 garlic cloves, finely sliced
6 eggs
salt and freshly ground
  black pepper

You can place the frying pan under the grill to cook the top of the tortilla instead of flipping it.

Something about a tortilla makes me smile. Whether it's the thought of Spain or sharing tapas with friends, I really love it. It can be eaten hot or cold and is great as a quick lunch or in lunchboxes the next day. You can add lovely flavours – chorizo, bacon, mushroom or spinach – just don't overfill and definitely don't overcook it. You want that little eggy wobble in the middle. It's also great between two slices of bread – yes, I've done that too.

Heat a good glug of olive oil in a large frying pan over a low-medium heat and fry the sweet potatoes for 10–15 minutes until softened. You can put a lid on the pan to help speed up this process. You don't want the potatoes to colour, so keep an eye on the heat. Flip them over from time to time, but try not to break them up too much. You may need to cook them in batches, depending on the size of your pan. Remove from the heat and transfer the sweet potatoes to a bowl or plate.

Put the frying pan back over a medium heat and add more oil. Add the onions and pepper and fry for 4–5 minutes until they start to soften and colour slightly. Add the garlic and fry for a further 3–4 minutes until soft. Remove the pan from the heat.

Crack the eggs into a large bowl, season with salt and pepper and whisk together. Gently tip in the cooked sweet potato slices and the onions, pepper and garlic. Mix very gently.

Place the frying pan back over a low heat – if there is not enough oil, add a little more oil, then pour in the egg mixture. Gently shuffle so the mixture is evenly distributed and cook for 15–20 minutes.

To flip the tortilla, place a plate on top of the pan and carefully turn the tortilla out. Then slide the tortilla back into the pan with the uncooked side facing down. Cook for a further 5 minutes until golden. The centre should still be slightly wobbly – if you prefer your eggs more cooked, then leave for a further few minutes.

Slide the tortilla out on to a plate and serve warm and wobbly with crusty bread.

Lemony tomato, pepper + cod parcels

SERVES 2

1 red pepper, deseeded and
   chopped into small pieces
handful of mangetout
thumb-sized piece of fresh
   ginger, peeled and sliced
   into matchsticks
1 garlic clove, crushed
zest and juice of 1 lemon
2 cod fillets or loin, skin on
olive oil
2 vines of cherry tomatoes,
   with about 6–8 tomatoes
   on each
small handful of fresh dill,
   chopped
salt and freshly ground
   black pepper
100g cooked couscous,
   to serve

Anything seafood I am there! These little parcels of tastiness are so fast to make, and you can put everything in together, so it's minimal fuss, mess and prep. If cod is too expensive or you can't get it, then go for another sustainable white fish such as haddock or pollock which both work beautifully. The little parcels make you feel quite fancy too, plus all the veg in there means you're getting those vitamins and minerals to keep you fighting fit even though you may not feel it.

Preheat the oven to 160°C fan (180°C/350°F/Gas Mark 4).

Put the pepper, mangetout, ginger, garlic, lemon zest and juice and some salt and pepper in a bowl. Give it a really good mix, then add the cod and gently rub the marinade into the fish.

Place a large piece of foil on a flat baking tray and drizzle over some oil. Place the cod on top and tip over the lemony vegetables. Top each piece of cod with one of the tomato vines. Drizzle over a little more oil. Fold up the edges of the foil and roll the top down to make a large sealed parcel.

Bake for 15 minutes – if the cod is thick it may need slightly longer. The fish should flake away easily when cooked.

Remove from the oven and undo the parcel. Gently lift out the cod and vegetables, place on top of some cooked couscous and sprinkle over some freshly chopped dill.

Chicken sausage, butternut squash + burrata lasagne

MAKES 4 REALLY BIG PORTIONS OR 6 SMALLER ONES

10 chicken sausages (I used Heck)
olive oil
knob of butter
1 red onion, finely chopped
½ butternut squash, peeled, halved lengthways and cut into 4–5mm slices
1 courgette, cut into 4–5mm slices
2 garlic cloves, finely chopped
500ml chicken stock
250g ricotta cheese
200g baby spinach
small bunch of fresh basil, leaves only
1 packet of fresh lasagne sheets (12–15 sheets)
2 balls of burrata
30g Parmesan cheese, grated
salt and freshly ground black pepper
cucumber, Little Gem lettuce and balsamic vinegar, to serve

Now this is a masterpiece, even if I do say so myself. Not heavy with cream, but packed with vegetables, lighter than the usual lasagne with chicken sausages and oh my goodness, the stretchy, stringy burrata is next level. You can use any cheese you like – mozzarella works well too – and pork sausages with fennel seeds are also a delight. Portion it up and freeze for the perfect belly-filling, smile-inducing meal on a rainy, grey day.

Preheat the oven to 160°C fan (180°C/350°F/Gas Mark 4).

Squeeze the meat out of the sausage skins so you have nuggets of chicken sausage.

Add a glug of oil and the butter to a large frying pan over a medium heat, then add the chicken sausage meat. Bash about for 4–5 minutes while it cooks to break it down slightly. Add the onion and fry for about 3 minutes, then add the butternut squash, courgette and garlic and fry for 5–6 minutes until the butternut squash starts to soften and everything has a little colour.

Pour in the stock and allow to bubble and reduce down slightly. Stir through the ricotta so you have a lovely thick, creamy sauce. Drop in the spinach leaves and mix until completely wilted. Season well with salt and pepper, then tear in the fresh basil leaves. Try not to break up the butternut squash slices too much.

Spread some of the liquid sauce from the mixture over the base of a deep ovenproof dish, then add a layer of fresh lasagne sheets. Now spoon over a good layer of the chicken sausage mixture and tear over some of the oozing burrata. Add another layer of lasagne sheets, then more of the chicken sausage mixture and more burrata.

Continue until all of the mixture has been used up, keeping a little liquid sauce for the topping and finishing with a layer of lasagne sheets. Spoon the reserved sauce over the top, dot over the last of the burrata and scatter over the grated Parmesan.

Bake for 25–35 minutes until the cheese is bubbling and golden on top and the lasagne sheets are cooked through. Leave to stand for 10 minutes before serving. Serve with cucumber and Little Gem lettuce drizzled with balsamic vinegar.

You can portion and freeze this for another dinner time!

Image overleaf →

Everything-in Bolognese

SERVES 4

olive oil
2 red onions, chopped
150g chestnut mushrooms,
  chopped
1 red pepper, deseeded and
  chopped
2 red chillies, sliced
2 celery sticks, sliced
1 large carrot, peeled and
  chopped
3 rashers of smoked streaky
  bacon, sliced into lardons
  and skin removed
150g chorizo, halved
  lengthways and cut into
  3mm slices
4 garlic cloves, finely diced
100g mixed pitted olives,
  halved lengthways
500g beef mince (5% fat)
2 x 400g tins chopped
  tomatoes
1 heaped tbsp tomato purée
175ml red wine
2 beef stock cubes
2 tsp dried oregano
1 Parmesan rind
400g linguine
bunch of fresh basil
splash of Worcestershire sauce
salt and freshly ground
  black pepper
Parmesan, grated,
  to serve (optional)

Spaghetti Bolognese is the ultimate midweek dinner. I remember my Nan making it for the first time and she couldn't quite get to grips with the recipe as she had never made it before. Weird, as now it's such a staple for many and everyone has developed their own way of making it. Mine is adding whatever I can find, including olives, which add a lovely saltiness, and chorizo for a little kick. I hope I don't upset anyone with my not-so-traditional interpretation, but what I love about cooking is that it really is down to personal preference and taste. So, go for it!

Add a glug of oil to a large saucepan over a medium heat. Add the red onions, mushrooms, pepper, chillies, celery and carrot and stir. Add the bacon and chorizo to the pan along with garlic and olives and fry for 4–5 minutes until the onions start to colour and the bacon is cooked.

Add the beef mince and break up with a wooden spoon. Cook until it starts to turn a lovely brown colour, then pour in the tinned tomatoes and squirt in the tomato purée. Use the red wine to swirl out the tins of tomatoes and add. Give everything a really good stir.

Then drop in the stock cubes, dried oregano and the Parmesan rind. Stir and add some salt and pepper. Cover and cook for about 1½ hours until everything is thick, bubbling and beautiful.

Meanwhile, bring a large saucepan of salted water to the boil and cook the linguine according to the packet instructions (normally about 8 minutes). Drain, reserving a little of the pasta cooking water, and pile into bowls.

If the Bolognese sauce is too thick, add a little pasta water to the sauce. Add the Worcestershire sauce and season to taste – you may not need too much salt as the olives and Parmesan are quite salty. Remove the Parmesan rind and divide the sauce between the bowls of linguine.

Tear over some fresh basil leaves and grate over some Parmesan should you wish.

Goat's cheese, smoked salmon + asparagus filo tart

SERVES 4–6

6–8 sheets of ready-made
   filo pastry
50g unsalted butter, melted
250g fine asparagus
5 eggs
100ml double cream
100ml whole milk
small bunch of fresh
   flat-leaf parsley
200g baby spinach
5 spring onions, trimmed
   and finely chopped
200g smoked salmon
250g soft goat's cheese
salt and freshly ground
   black pepper

You can also make individual tarts in muffin tins, just reduce the cooking time to 15–20 minutes.

A gorgeous spring/summer tart that's light enough for lunch and also perfect if you are not too hungry, but know you have to have something to eat. This happens a lot to me, so a dish like this in the fridge or even made into little individual tarts is ideal. Not a fan of fish, then swap it out for extra vegetables, ham hock or even more cheese. You can use shortcrust pastry too – I always keep pastry in the freezer for recipes like this.

Preheat the oven to 160°C fan (180°C/350°F/Gas Mark 4).

Brush a 25cm flan or quiche tin with melted butter and then lay in the first layer of filo pastry. Brush this with melted butter and lay in the second layer, then brush with more melted butter. Repeat with the filo and butter until there are no gaps in the pastry, the tin is covered, and you have lots of lovely jagged edges sticking up. You will have to arrange the sheets at different angles – about 6–8 sheets of pastry should work. Brush the last layer of pastry with butter and bake for 8–10 minutes until the filo starts to turn golden and crispy. Remove from the oven and set aside.

Bend the asparagus spears until they snap – this is the bit that is too woody to eat – then blanch for 2 minutes in boiling water.

Mix the eggs, cream, milk and some salt and pepper together in a jug. Finely chop the parsley and stir through.

Layer up the spinach, asparagus and spring onions in the baked filo pastry case and tear the smoked salmon over the top. Pour over the egg mixture and top with slices of the goat's cheese. Very carefully transfer the filled filo pastry case to the oven. (You may find it easier to put the flan tin on a flat baking tray and pour the egg mixture into the pastry while it is in the oven – just be careful not to burn yourself.)

Bake for 25–30 minutes until the egg is just set with a slight wobble and the filo is golden brown – if it starts to catch, simply cover it with foil.

Serve warm on its own or with a heap of salad.

Pork meatballs with creamy mustard broccoli + orzo

SERVES 4

400g lean pork mince
1 tsp dried sage
olive oil
200g chestnut mushrooms,
   sliced
2 leeks, sliced
3 garlic cloves, finely
   chopped or crushed
½ tsp chilli flakes
200ml cider or chicken stock
200ml double cream
3 heaped tsp wholegrain
   mustard
1 small broccoli, broken
   into small florets
200g orzo
1 tsp cornflour (optional)
salt and freshly ground
   black pepper

I think this recipe came from something I had to make in GCSE food technology. Cream, wholegrain mustard and pasta must be engrained in my brain somewhere! I serve this in massive portions with loads of orzo which, to be honest, I'm a little bit obsessed with – I think it's the texture. If you can, use a really good-quality pork mince, but turkey mince works well too. The pork alongside the creamy tangy sauce and big broccoli florets makes this wholesome, hot and so needed on those days when you need your food to give you a big hug. Serve with tagliatelle or buttery mash or even rice if you fancy.

Put the pork mince and dried sage in a bowl and season with a pinch of salt and pepper. Give everything a good squeeze together and form into meatballs roughly the size of a golf ball.

Heat a glug of oil in a large frying pan over a medium-high heat and pop in the meatballs. Cook, turning them over until coloured on all sides. Remove from the pan and set aside – they will finish cooking in the sauce.

Add a little more oil to the same pan over a medium heat and fry the mushrooms and leeks for 3–4 minutes until they start to soften and turn golden. Then add the garlic and chilli flakes and stir for 1–2 minutes.

Pour in the cider or stock and allow to bubble for a couple of minutes. Add the double cream and stir, then mix through the wholegrain mustard and drop in the broccoli. Add the meatballs to the bubbling sauce and allow to fully cook through while you cook the orzo.

Bring a large saucepan of salted water to the boil and add the orzo. Cook according to the packet instructions, then drain, reserving some of the pasta cooking water.

Add a little of the reserved pasta water to the meatballs and broccoli or if you prefer a thicker sauce, mix the cornflour with the pasta water before mixing it through.

Season to taste and serve the meatballs and sauce heaped on top of the hot orzo.

Do not add the cornflour directly to the sauce.

Pesto gnocchi gratin

SERVES 4

500g shop-bought or
   homemade gnocchi
   (page 109)
200ml double cream
2 tbsp mascarpone cheese
about 3–4 tbsp sun-dried
   tomato pesto
small bunch of fresh basil
1 x 125g ball mozzarella
150g Cheddar cheese, grated
salt and freshly ground
   black pepper

Need comfort food? Then here you go. Carbs on carbs on carbs, covered in cheese and baked in the oven. You can even make your own gnocchi if you want – it's simpler than you think and so satisfying (see page 109). A word of advice – give this a moment to cool before getting it in your gob. I learned the hard way, but still went back a second and third time. You'll want to eat it straight out the dish with all those crispy, drippy bits – do it.

Preheat the oven to 170°C fan (190°C/375°F/Gas Mark 5).

Bring a large saucepan of lightly salted water to the boil. Add the gnocchi and cook for about 2 minutes – it needs to be slightly undercooked. Drain, reserving a little of the pasta water, and set aside.

In another saucepan, heat the cream over a medium heat until almost bubbling. (It may thicken up too.) Stir in the mascarpone cheese, then mix through the pesto. Season to taste with salt and pepper.

Tip the gnocchi into the sauce and stir through. Tear the basil leaves from the stems and mix through. Tear up the mozzarella ball and fold this through the gnocchi. Pour into an ovenproof dish and sprinkle over the grated Cheddar. Bake for 20–25 minutes until the cheese is melted and golden and it is bubbling beautifully around the edges.

Remove from the oven and set aside for 10 minutes before serving. It will be like lava – the tastiest lava you've ever eaten!

Spicy chicken + cashew traybake

SERVES 4

olive oil
8 chicken thighs (either
    skinless and deboned or
    with bones in and skin on)
1 yellow pepper, deseeded
    and sliced
1 red pepper, deseeded
    and sliced
1 red onion, chopped
2 red chillies, finely chopped
10 cherry tomatoes, halved
6 garlic cloves, peeled
3 sweet potatoes, scrubbed
    and cut into wedges
150g chorizo, skin removed
    and cut into 3mm slices
drizzle of honey
150g green or black olives,
    pitted
200g cashew nuts
soured cream, to serve

One of those wonderful one-tray, bang-it-in meals. You get so much lovely flavour from chicken thighs and they don't dry out like their breasty mates. Skip the potatoes and serve with rice or couscous instead or shred it all up and whack it in a flour tortilla for a little fajita vibe. Lazy cooking at its best for when you really can't be arsed. (You can even skip the making your own seasoning bit if you want – just get a readymade one and sprinkle to your heart's content.)

Preheat the oven to 160°C fan (180°C/350°F/Gas Mark 4).

Add all the Cajun spice mix ingredients to a clean, dry jar, put on the lid and give it a really good shake. You will have more seasoning than you need for this recipe, but it will keep for about six months.

Drizzle some olive oil over a large baking tray and swirl it around to coat the tray.

Put the peppers, onion, chillies, tomatoes, garlic, sweet potatoes and chorizo into a large bowl. Drizzle over a little oil and give it a good rub and mix. Sprinkle over ½ tablespoon of the Cajun spice mix and give it another good mix. Tip the spiced veg on to the prepared tray and spread out evenly across the tray.

Add the chicken to the bowl and rub in another 1 tablespoon of Cajun spice mix, really massaging it into the chicken. Place the chicken on top of the prepared veg and cook for 15 minutes.

CAJUN SPICE MIX:

2 tbsp smoked paprika

½ tbsp cayenne pepper

½ tsp salt

1 tsp chilli flakes

1 tbsp garlic salt

1 tbsp freshly ground
   black pepper

½ tbsp onion powder

½ tbsp dried oregano

½ tbsp dried thyme

½ tbsp cumin seeds

Remove the tray from the oven and, using a fish slice or spatula, give everything a good mix. Return to the oven for a further 15 minutes.

Remove the tray from the oven, drizzle over the honey, sprinkle over the olives and cashews and mix lightly. Check the chicken and return to the oven for a further 10 minutes. Cooking the chicken skin-side up will give crispy skin if you're using chicken with the skin on.

Check the chicken is cooked, especially if you are using thighs with the bones in, there should be no pink flesh visible.

Serve the traybake as it is with a bit of everything.

Or serve with soured cream on top if you need it!

Image overleaf →

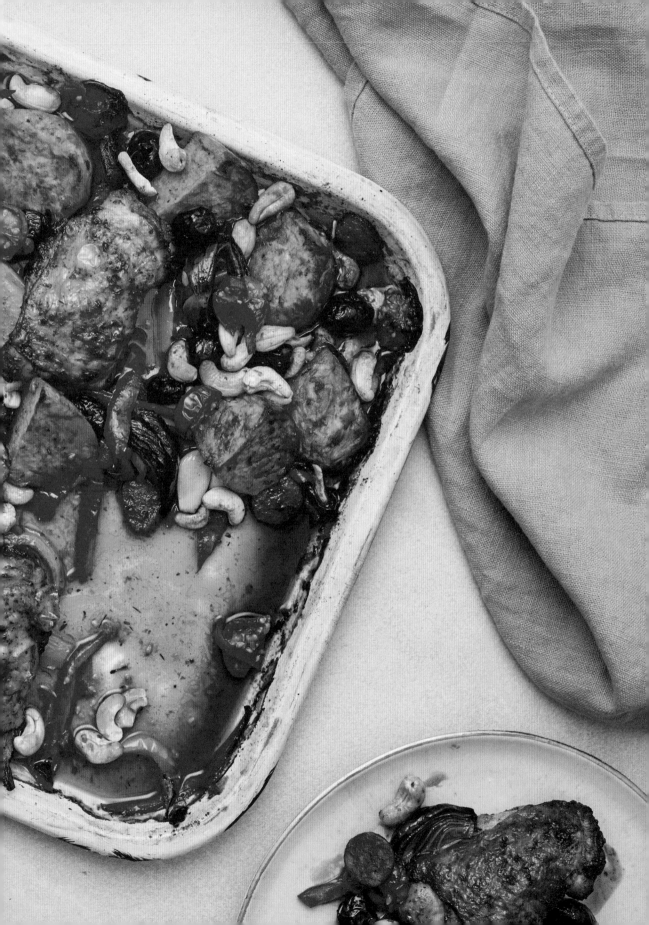

The best hash browns — kedgeree style!

SERVES 2

2 unbleached smoked
   haddock fillets
500ml whole milk
knob of butter
1 bay leaf
white vinegar
2 eggs
few sprigs of fresh coriander

HASH BROWNS:
1 large potato, peeled
   (I used Maris piper)
1 sweet potato, peeled
2 banana (echalion) shallots,
   finely sliced
1 tsp cumin seeds
½ tsp paprika
½ tsp chilli flakes
½ tsp hot madras curry
   powder, plus extra
   to serve
25g Parmesan cheese,
   finely grated
1 egg
olive oil
knob of butter
salt and freshly ground
   black pepper

When my depression was at a real peak a few years ago, I got a little bit obsessed with hash browns. You know, the triangle frozen ones. I would go and see my parents and my mam would be making a cooked breakfast, but I'd just want hash browns and salt. I love the fancy ones too, proper American style, so I played with creating my own version – keeping the frozen ones for really grey days. The mild curry flavour and haddock topping reminded me of a kedgeree, but these hash browns are also great with crispy bacon, fried portobello mushrooms or on their own as a meal accompaniment.

Preheat the oven to 160°C fan (180°C/350°F/Gas Mark 4).

Place the haddock pieces skin-side down in a shallow, ovenproof dish and pour over the milk so it just about covers them. Add the butter and bay leaf. Cook for about 20 minutes until the fish is cooked and flakes easily.

Meanwhile, make the hash browns. Coarsely grate both potatoes and squeeze out any excess liquid. If you find this hard, you can put the grated potatoes in a clean cloth and twist until it squeezes out any liquid. Transfer to a bowl. Add the shallots, cumin seeds, paprika, chilli flakes, curry powder, a really good pinch of salt and pepper, the Parmesan and finally crack in the egg. Give everything a really good mix together.

You might want to get your hands in to squeeze the mixture together.

Set a frying pan over a medium heat and add a glug of olive oil and the butter. Wait until the butter has melted, then take a small handful of the potato mixture, flatten it down into a patty and add to the pan. You can fry the hash browns in batches of two or three patties. Fry for 3–4 minutes before flipping them over – don't worry if they break slightly, they're not supposed to be held together like a cake! Fry for a further couple of minutes on the other side. Keep warm in the oven while you cook the remaining hash browns.

You can either wrap the uncooked patties and keep in the fridge for a day or cook off and reheat when you want to eat them. The uncooked patties can also be wrapped in greaseproof paper and frozen separately for up to a month.

To poach the eggs, bring a saucepan of water to the boil and reduce the heat so it is not vigorously bubbling. Add a good splash of vinegar. Use a spoon to spin the water in a whirlpool. Crack the eggs into a small bowl, one at a time, then, one at a time, gently pour the eggs into the centre of the whirlpool. Cook for 3–4 minutes until the whites have set. Lift out with a slotted spoon or spatula and place on a board with kitchen paper to drain.

To serve, place two hash browns per person on a plate, lift the fish out of the milk with a slotted spoon and allow to drain off, then lay on top of the hash browns. Top with a poached egg, a couple of sprigs of fresh coriander, a sprinkle of curry powder and some freshly ground black pepper. Let's hope the yolk is nice and runny!

Arancini (risotto balls)

SERVES 2, depending on how much leftover risotto you have

small bunch of fresh flat-leaf parsley, finely chopped
1x 125g ball mozzarella, drained and cut into small cubes
50g Parmesan cheese, finely grated
about 300g Mushroom, Spinach & Sweetcorn Risotto (page 148) or Smoky Bean Chilli (page 139)
100g plain flour
2 eggs
splash of whole milk
100g panko or homemade breadcrumbs
sunflower oil
salt and freshly ground black pepper
Spicy sriracha mayo (page 50), to serve

Serve with spicy mayo – yum!

As much as I love cooking, sometimes I just don't want to, and I know that's how others feel too. Especially if you have that grey cloud, anxiety is high or you're just low on energy. So, I've tried to create a couple of recipes that can be taken from one. This is one of them. Hopefully this means that the effort is spread out and cooking becomes a little less arduous on those bad days. These risotto balls also freeze well – just defrost in the fridge before frying. As always, you can swap the cheese in the middle or just leave it out.

Mix the parsley, mozzarella and Parmesan together and season with a little salt and pepper.

Take a handful of leftover risotto and flatten it in the palm of your hand. Place a cube of the mozzarella and Parmesan mixture in the middle, then fold the risotto up, encasing the cheese so it is fully covered with no gaps or holes. Repeat with the remaining risotto – you can make the arancini whatever size you like, from golf-ball to tennis-ball sized depending how hungry you are! Place the arancini in the fridge.

Add the flour to a bowl, mix the eggs with the milk in a second bowl and add the breadcrumbs to a third. Remove the risotto balls from the fridge and, one by one, carefully roll the risotto balls in the flour, then dip into the egg mixture and finally coat in breadcrumbs.

Preheat the oven to 160°C fan (180°C/350°F/Gas Mark 4).

Heat either a deep-fat fryer or a saucepan with 7.5-10cm sunflower oil to 190°C (375°F) or until a cube of bread floats to the top and turns golden brown when dropped in.

In batches of two or three, depending how big your balls are, carefully lower the arancini into the hot oil with a slotted spoon and fry for 3–4 minutes until golden brown all over. My arancini were quite large, so I finished them off in the oven for 5–7 minutes until piping hot and gooey in the middle.

Charred corn + smoked chilli cornbread

SERVES UP TO 8

100g sweetcorn (I used frozen)
360ml whole milk
30ml lemon juice
100g plain flour
250g coarse polenta
   (cornmeal)
2 tsp baking powder
1 tbsp light soft brown sugar
1 tsp salt
1 tsp freshly ground black
   pepper
½ tsp smoked chilli powder
1½ tsp smoked paprika
100g Manchego cheese,
   grated
50g unsalted butter, melted
2 red chillies, finely chopped
4 spring onions, finely chopped
2 eggs
50g Cheddar cheese, grated

This really simple recipe goes well with soups and chilli or is perfect just warm with butter. It's not bread as you know it, so no kneading or proving, but a lovely, slightly odd texture that you can really add whatever you like to. It's pretty forgiving too, so have a play with flavours – obviously mine is spicy with chilli. Also, if you have one, you get to use a kitchen blowtorch and feel pretty badass for a bit!

Preheat the oven to 200°C fan (220°C/425°F/Gas Mark 7) and line a 20cm square or rectangular baking tin with fairly high sides with greaseproof paper.

Scatter the sweetcorn over a baking tray and use a kitchen blowtorch to lightly torch the corn so you get some charring. (If you don't have a blowtorch, you can lightly fry the sweetcorn or just leave it as it is.) Transfer to a food processor and very roughly blitz the sweetcorn – you want a rough texture so don't overdo it.

Pour the milk and lemon juice into a jug, mix together and set aside. This makes buttermilk – it will thicken and look slightly curdled, but that's fine.

Put the flour, polenta, baking powder, sugar, salt, pepper, chilli and paprika in a large bowl and mix together. Add the grated Manchego and stir though with a blunt knife.

Make a well in the middle of the dry ingredients and pour in the butter, chillies, spring onions, buttermilk and eggs and mix together until you have a smooth batter. Add the blitzed sweetcorn and fold through. Pour the batter into the prepared tin and bake for 35–45 minutes. Top with the Cheddar after 25 minutes.

Remove from the oven, leave to cool in the tin for 10 minutes, then remove and set on a wire rack. Cut into wedges and serve warm.

Image overleaf →

Mushroom, artichoke + tarragon stroganoff

SERVES 4-6

olive oil
knob of butter
1 large onion, chopped
4 garlic cloves
500g mixed mushrooms,
    such as chestnut, button,
    portobello, closed cup,
    porcini or oyster
290g jarred artichokes
    (I used the ones in garlic
    and herb oil)
1 tsp smoked paprika
1 tsp cayenne pepper
½ tsp smoked seaweed
    powder (optional)
1 tsp English mustard
200ml white wine
250ml vegetable stock
small bunch of fresh tarragon
200ml double cream
juice of ½ lemon
splash of Worcestershire sauce
salt and freshly ground
    black pepper
cooked wholegrain rice,
    to serve

If you want meaty without meat, then this is the dish for you. I love mushrooms and the fact this has all the mushrooms in it. We are so lucky to get some wonderful varieties during fungi season and this recipe makes the best of them. Artichokes may be odd to look at and normally used for antipasti, but I love the almost tang you get from them in this dish. I use jarred, but you can use fresh if you wish.

Place a large saucepan or frying pan over a low-medium heat and add a glug of oil and the butter. Add the onion and cook for about 3 minutes until it starts to pale slightly, but not colour. Squash the garlic with the back of a knife and chop. Add to the onion.

Chop any large mushrooms or tear them up. Keep any button or small mushrooms whole so you have varying sizes for texture. Add these to the pan and keep stirring until softened. This should take about 5 minutes.

Add a little of the artichoke oil to the pan, if you are using artichokes in oil. Then add the paprika, cayenne pepper, seaweed powder, if using, and mustard. Stir through.

Drain off the oil from the artichokes and add the artichokes to the pan – try not to break up the chunks. Add the white wine and allow to bubble and reduce very slightly before adding the stock. Tear in the tarragon, stir and leave to bubble away for a couple of minutes.

Once everything is looking hot, cooked and lovely, reduce the heat to low and stir through the cream and lemon juice and mix. Season with Worcestershire sauce and salt and pepper, taste and allow to heat through. Serve with wholegrain rice.

This freezes well for up to one month. Defrost before heating in a pan.

The best potato salad

SERVES 4-5

500g Jersey royal or salad
  potatoes, larger ones halved
150g smoked streaky bacon,
  thinly sliced
4 spring onions, finely sliced
  (green bits too)
100g gherkins or cornichons,
  chopped
small bunch of fresh flat-leaf
  parsley, finely chopped
2 tsp wholegrain mustard
3 tbsp mayonnaise
zest of 1 lemon, plus about 1
  tbsp juice
salt and freshly ground
  black pepper

OK, second best, as Burnie taught me all I know about potato salad! BBQ? Potato Salad. Picnic? Potato Salad. Hungry? Potato Salad! Get the gist? Don't save this for the summer though, it makes a great change from chips or mash or just potatoes. You want to make sure the bacon is super crispy to contrast with the crushed potatoes and please make sure you get them almost mushy as that's how they are best. I always have gherkins in the fridge – one for the salad, one for me.

Bring a saucepan of salted water to the boil over a high heat. Once at a rolling boil, carefully add the potatoes and boil for about 20 minutes until soft and crushable with a fork. Drain and tip into a large bowl.

Meanwhile, add the bacon to a dry frying pan over a medium-high heat and fry until crispy.

Add the spring onions, gherkins, parsley and cooked bacon to the potatoes and mix together. Dollop in the mustard and mayonnaise then fold through – the potatoes should break down slightly. Add the lemon zest and juice and season with salt and pepper to taste.

Crunchy coleslaw

SERVES 6-8

¼ red cabbage, finely sliced
¼ white cabbage, finely sliced
2 large carrots, peeled and
    finely sliced
1 red onion, finely sliced
3 celery sticks, finely sliced
1 eating apple, grated
zest of 1 lemon and juice of ½
small bunch of fresh flat-leaf
    parsley, finely chopped
3 heaped tbsp mayonnaise
1 tbsp wholegrain mustard
50g pumpkin seeds, toasted
salt and freshly ground
    black pepper

I do sometimes worry that side dishes get left out, so I wanted to make a coleslaw that would take a little bit more of a starring role. You want texture and crunch as well as flavour and this gives both, plus the apple adds a surprise sweetness. Enjoy it in sandwiches, next to your burger (like we do at the pub) or have a heap of it with my Ultimate chicken nuggets (see page 50). Sprinkle on some toasted seeds and you've got yourself a special side dish.

Put all the prepared vegetables and apple, lemon zest and parsley in a large bowl, get your hands in and mix around so all the ingredients are evenly distributed.

Whack in the mayonnaise, lemon juice and wholegrain mustard, season with salt and pepper and give everything a good mix and squish together with your hands. Transfer to a fancy bowl for serving and sprinkle with the toasted pumpkin seeds.

You can also use this coleslaw for topping burgers, adding to sandwiches, taking to barbecues or just as a sexy little salad option. It will keep covered in the fridge for up to three days.

Keep-your-hands-busy cooking

SAVOURY:

Blue cheese, pesto and walnut bread – 85

Mozzarella-stuffed burgers and
deep-fried pickles – 87

Tear and share turmeric, cumin and
Gorgonzola bread – 90

Khachapuri – 92

Cauliflower, squash kale and cheese pasties – 96

Beetroot, feta and nigella seed scones – 99

Courgette, chickpea and halloumi falafel – 100

Bacon, cheese and chive croquettes – 101

My type of pizza – 104

Salmon and edamame bean fishcakes – 107

Homemade gnocchi – 109

SWEET:

White chocolate, cardamom, almond
and lemon pastry twists – 110

Rocky road cookies – 112

Apricot and almond decorated biscuits – 113

Honey and lemon round challah – 116

Swedish cinnamon buns (Kanelbullar) – 119

Apricot and amaretto pastel de nata – 121

Chocolate caramel babka – 123

Apple and pear sweet 'dauphinoise' – 125

Gingerbread house – 128

ONE OF my first indicators of anxiety is my hands; I wring my hands, I fiddle with my rings, I tap and fidget even more than usual. I have to be doing something all the time – my attention span is bad at the best of times, but if I'm feeling anxious then the need to be busy is through the roof.

Having recently been diagnosed with ADHD (attention deficit hyperactivity disorder), a lot of this makes sense, as I just cannot sit still. My family and friends call me the Bumble Bee as I buzz around doing everything, but not actually doing much. I also get things done, just in my own time and way, often doing several other things along the way and having to be reminded to stay on task!

So much at the moment brings on anxiety, whether it is worry, panic, not sleeping enough, intrusive thoughts or just the pressures of day-to-day life. This chapter is all about keeping your hands busy through cooking and baking. The therapeutic ways of kneading bread, making pastry from scratch or shaping patties. This is something I have always spoken about – the calming feel and touch of food. Using my hands to create and take me to that happy place. It's funny as I find it so hard to concentrate, but give me some dough and that's me all in.

These are great recipes to make with kids too – to introduce them to the mindful pleasure of making things to eat. Transforming a handful of basic, simple ingredients into something edible and beautiful is very satisfying for both the stomach and the mind.

Blue cheese, pesto + walnut bread

MAKES 1 BIG LOAF

350g strong white bread flour,
   plus extra for dusting
7g fine sea salt
½ tbsp caster sugar
7g instant yeast
200g walnuts, roughly
   chopped
250–300ml lukewarm water
olive oil
2 heaped tbsp green pesto
200g Stilton cheese
1 egg, beaten

Making bread is a form of therapy for me. The whole process, from start to finish, is methodical, calming and cathartic. With so many types of bread and things you can do with it, it was hard to choose just a couple of recipes, but blue cheese was always going to find its way in. You don't need a lot for a big flavour impact and it really works with the pesto. If you're not a fan, then swap it for Cheddar or something a little different like Jarlsberg and you can also leave out the nuts, if you wish.

Sift the flour into the bowl of a free-standing electric mixer fitted with the dough hook. Make a well in the middle of the flour. Put the salt and sugar on one side of the flour and the yeast on the opposite side. Add the chopped walnuts to the well. Slowly pour the lukewarm water into the well (do not add it all at once in case you do not need it all). Turn the mixer on to a low speed and mix until all the flour has been incorporated, adding more water if needed. You want a soft, slightly sticky dough.

You can then either turn out the dough on to a lightly floured work surface and knead for 10–12 minutes by hand or mix for 7–8 minutes on medium speed with the dough hook. The dough should be smooth and elastic.

Shape the dough into a ball and put it into a large, lightly oiled bowl. Cover with clingfilm and leave to rise in a warm place for about 2 hours until the dough has at least doubled in size.

Continued overleaf →

Knock the air out of the risen dough with your knuckles, then turn out on to a lightly oiled work surface. Roll out the dough into a rectangle about 20 x 15cm, then spread over the pesto and crumble over the Stilton. From one short side, roll up the dough into a large Swiss-roll shape, then transfer on to a lightly floured piece of greaseproof paper on a baking tray, with the seam on the bottom. With a very sharp knife or bread blade, slash diagonal lines across the bread so you can see at least some of the pesto and cheese in the openings. Place in a large plastic bag (keeping some air in) and put in a warm place to rise for 45 minutes to 1 hour until the dough has doubled in size and springs back when poked.

Preheat the oven to 180°C fan (200°C/400°F/Gas Mark 6) and place a high-sided tray in the bottom of the oven to heat up.

Remove the loaf from the bag but keep it on the lined tray and brush the whole loaf with the beaten egg. Bake for 30–40 minutes and as you close the oven door, pour a jug of cold water into the hot tray to create steam. Check the bread is cooked by tapping the bottom – it should sound hollow.

Remove the bread from the oven and place on a wire rack. The cheese and pesto should be living their best life and oozing all over the place! Best eaten on the day it's made, or it can be stored in a tin and warmed in the oven the next day.

Perfect sliced and toasted too!

Mozzarella-stuffed burgers + deep-fried pickles

MAKES 4 BIG OL' BURGERS OR 6 SLIDERS

BURGERS:
500g beef mince (10% fat)
1 garlic clove, crushed
1 small red chilli, finely diced
½ red onion, finely diced
good splash of
   Worcestershire sauce
1 egg yolk
10cm piece of chorizo,
   skin removed and diced
1 x 125g ball mozzarella,
   drained (or string cheese
   works brilliantly)
olive oil
salt and freshly ground
   black pepper

DEEP-FRIED PICKLES:
sunflower oil
2 heaped tbsp plain flour,
   plus 2 tbsp for coating
1 tsp bicarbonate soda
about 100ml soda water
4 large gherkins (we call
   them wallies!)

TO SERVE:
4–6 burger buns (depending
   on size of burgers)
lettuce
cucumber, sliced
Spicy sriracha mayo
   (page 50)

Burgers have really got **BIG** over the last few years in both size and stature. No longer a quick drive-through pick-up, but gourmet, alternative and with pretty much every filling you can imagine. I think making your own burgers at home is the way forward and it's so easy. Plus, the flavours you can get and play with are unlimited. These are a simple version that work every time and you get to use one of those weird Christmas presents you got from Secret Santa – the burger press that you always wanted! Great for BBQ season and with lamb mince too.

To make the burgers, put the beef mince, garlic, chilli, red onion, Worcestershire sauce, egg yolk and chorizo in a large bowl and season with salt and pepper. Get your hands in there and give everything a really good squash and squeeze together. You want the mixture to be evenly combined so you have a bit of all the tasty stuff! At this point you can fry a tiny bit off to taste for seasoning.

Chop the mozzarella into four or six pieces, depending on the size burgers you are getting in your gob!

Roll the beef mince mixture into 4–6 equal-sized balls, then flatten down into patty shapes. Place a lump of mozzarella into the middle of each ball, then roll up the edges and squeeze together so the cheese is completely encased with no gaps. Flatten down again slightly into burger shapes. If you have a fancy burger press, then use that!

Heat a griddle pan over a high heat. Brush each burger with a little oil and place in the pan. Fry for about 3 minutes on each side. You want them to be nice and chargrilled. If you like your burgers a little more well done, you can finish them off in the oven at 160°C fan (180°C/350°F/Gas Mark 4) for 10 minutes.

Continued overleaf →

While the burgers are cooking, you can prep the pickles. Heat about 2.5–5cm of sunflower oil in a heavy-duty saucepan until about 190°C (375°F). If you don't have a thermometer, test the oil is ready by adding a cube of bread. If the oil is ready, it should sizzle, turn golden brown and float to the top.

Mix the 2 heaped tablespoons of plain flour with the bicarbonate soda in a bowl and add the soda water until you have a thick but smooth, bubbly batter. Allow to sit for a few minutes.

Slice the gherkins in half lengthways. Put the remaining plain flour in a bowl and dust the gherkins with the flour, then dip into the batter until they are completely coated. Very carefully, put the battered gherkins into the hot oil and fry for about 2 minutes on each side until golden brown and crispy as hell. Remove with a slotted spoon and place on some kitchen paper to drain any excess oil.

Slice the burger buns in half and lightly toast them, then add a dollop of spicy sriracha mayo on the bottom half. Top with a cheese-stuffed burger, then the salad – I use cucumber and lettuce, then add a deep-fried pickle and another little dollop of spicy mayo. Top with the other half of the bun and stick a burger stick through a second pickle and straight through the burger to hold it all together.

These burgers are great cooked on the BBQ too and you can add more cheese and bacon as you wish.

Tear + share turmeric, cumin + Gorgonzola bread

SERVES 4–8

240ml lukewarm whole milk
25g unsalted butter, melted
200g strong white bread flour
200g plain flour, plus extra
  for dusting
10g instant yeast
10g fine sea salt
1 tbsp golden caster sugar
2 tsp cumin seeds
2 tsp ground turmeric
2 eggs, 1 beaten for egg wash
olive oil, for greasing
300g Gorgonzola

Oh wow, these are stunning to look at and eat. They are light and fluffy and tasty and gooey and yellow. You may want to wear gloves for kneading and shaping the dough as the turmeric might stain just a little. You can make any shape out of the buns and try sticking a Camembert in the middle before baking so you can dip your bun straight into the gooey cheese.

Mix the warm milk and the melted butter together in a jug.

Combine both types of flour in the large bowl of a free-standing electric mixer fitted with the dough hook and make a well in the centre. Add the yeast to one side and the salt, sugar, cumin seeds and turmeric to the opposite side.

Add the egg to the well of the dry ingredients and pour three quarters of the warm milk and butter into the well, then mix on a low speed for about 2 minutes until all the flour has been incorporated. Increase the speed to medium. If the mixture is looking too dry, add some more warm milk and butter. Mix for about 8 minutes until you have a soft, stretchy dough that you can see through if held up to the light.

Lightly oil a large bowl, add the dough and cover it with clingfilm. Leave in a warm place to rise for about 2 hours or until doubled in size.

Line a baking tray with greaseproof paper and sprinkle with flour.

Lightly oil a work surface. Push your fingers into the risen dough to knock the air out, then turn the risen dough out on to the work surface and fold it over itself a couple of times. Divide the dough into 13 equal portions. Flatten each portion and place a teaspoon-sized piece of Gorgonzola into the middle, then pinch the bottom so it encloses the cheese completely. Turn over so the seam is on the bottom and create a cage with your hand with the dough ball underneath and roll so you get a smooth ball shape. Repeat with all thirteen pieces. Arrange in a square on the prepared baking tray with three x three balls on the outside, four balls inside that and one ball in the middle all spaced just slightly apart. Place the tray in a large bag, enclose the air inside and place somewhere warm for 45 minutes to 1 hour until the dough has doubled in size or springs back to touch.

Preheat the oven to 170°C fan (190°C/375°F/Gas Mark 5).

Brush each roll with the beaten egg and bake for 15–20 minutes until golden brown and risen. Leave to cool on a wire rack.

Tear and share while warm.

Best eaten on the day for sure!

Khachapuri

**MAKES 4 LARGE
OR 6 SMALLER
KHACHAPURI**

25g unsalted butter,
   at room temperature,
   plus a large knob
250ml warm whole milk
450g strong white bread flour
7g fine sea salt
20g golden caster sugar
7g instant yeast
2 tsp dried seaweed
oil
1 x 250g Camembert
1x 125g ball mozzarella,
   drained
150g ricotta
5–7 eggs, depending how
   many khachapuri you
   are making
freshly ground black pepper
small bunch of fresh chives,
   finely snipped
sea salt flakes

Someone told me these bread boats are the best thing I've ever made and, to be honest, I think they're up there. Not only because of the process, which is just lovely, but for the flavour, aesthetic and the all-important slo-mo, Boomerang, breaking the runny yolk shot. Mix up the cheese, add in some spice or different herbs and see how they make you smile.

Add the butter to the warm milk and allow it to melt.

Put the flour in a large mixing bowl and make a well in the middle. Put the salt and sugar on one side and the yeast on the opposite side – don't let the yeast touch the salt! Add the dried seaweed to the well in the middle.

If you are using a free-standing electric mixer, fit the dough hook and place the bowl underneath. Set to low speed and slowly pour about three quarters of the warm milk and butter into the well of the dry ingredients. Add more as necessary until you have a soft but not wet dough. Once all the flour has been incorporated, increase the speed slightly to low-medium and knead for 7–8 minutes.

If mixing by hand, add the milk and butter mixture a little at a time and use your fingers to bring the flour in from the edges. Once all the flour has been incorporated, turn the dough out on to a lightly oiled work surface and knead for 10–12 minutes. The dough should be smooth and elastic when pulled so you can see light through it.

Lightly oil a large bowl and shape the dough into the bowl. Cover with clingfilm and put in a warm place for 1–2 hours or until the dough has at least doubled in size.

While the dough is proving – towards the end of the prove – chop the Camembert into small pieces and add to a bowl, then tear the mozzarella into pieces and add to the Camembert. Spoon in the ricotta, crack in an egg and add a good pinch of black pepper. Mix together until evenly combined.

Preheat the oven to 200°C fan (220°C/425°F/Gas Mark 7) and place a large baking tray in the oven.

Once the dough has at least doubled in size, remove the clingfilm and use your knuckles to knock the air out of the dough, then turn out on to a lightly oiled work surface. Divide the dough into 4–6 equal pieces (this makes fairly big Khachapuri) or divide into smaller pieces if you want (I definitely wouldn't want these smaller!). Roll and shape the dough into ovals about 5mm thick and the size of a small plate. Roll up the edges so you create a raised border about 3–4cm high and pinch the ends together to create a boat-like bowl. Transfer to a piece of greaseproof paper with space in between.

Spoon the cheese mix into the middle of the dough boats so it is about level with the rolled edge, but within the border and smooth down.

Carefully remove the hot baking tray from the oven and slide the greaseproof paper with the filled dough on to it. Bake for 10–12 minutes until the cheese starts to melt and the dough begins to turn golden.

Remove from the oven and, using a spoon, create a well in the middle of the melting cheese, then crack in an egg. Repeat with all the Khachapuri then return to the oven for a further 5–8 minutes until the eggs have just set.

Remove from the oven and dot over the butter so it melts into the cheese and egg and brush the edges of the raised sides with a little more butter. Sprinkle with sea salt flakes and fresh chives. For the ultimate show, break the yolk with a fork and gently mix the yolk through the hot cheese just as you serve.

Eat hot and gooey — just be very careful not to burn your mouth!

Image overleaf →

Cauliflower, squash, kale + cheese pasties

MAKES 4 BIG ONES

400g homemade or
   shop-bought shortcrust
   pastry, chilled
1 cauliflower, broken
   into florets
½ butternut squash peeled,
   deseeded and cut into
   1cm pieces
large bunch of kale
40g butter
2 large shallots, chopped
2 garlic cloves, finely chopped
40g plain flour, plus extra
   for dusting
400ml whole milk
300g mature Cheddar cheese,
   grated
100g Parmesan cheese, grated
1 heaped tbsp wholegrain
   mustard
1 egg, beaten
salt and freshly ground
   black pepper

If cauliflower cheese on its own is good, then imagine what it's like encased in pastry. Well, imagine no more. These pasties are perfect to make if you have any leftover cauliflower cheese from your roast (no, I don't either), and you keep your hands even busier by making your own pastry. Crimp, fold and squeeze the edges with a fork and you have a little handheld snack, lunch or dinner. Comfort food, but with added pastry, because pastry and cheese makes everything better.

Preheat the oven to 170°C fan (190°C/375°F/Gas Mark 5) and remove the pastry from the fridge.

Bring a large pan of salted water to the boil and add the cauliflower and butternut squash. Boil for 6–8 minutes until starting to become tender.

Strip the kale leaves from the tough woody stalks, rip the leaves into 5cm pieces and drop into the boiling water for about 1 minute to wilt down slightly. Drain and set aside.

Melt the butter in a saucepan over a medium heat, add the shallots and garlic, cook for a couple of minutes, then add the flour, mixing constantly for 2–3 minutes. Gradually pour in the milk, continually stirring over a low–medium heat until the sauce is smooth and thick enough to coat the back of a wooden spoon. Add both cheeses and stir until melted. Stir through the wholegrain mustard and season well with salt and pepper.

Tip the cooked cauliflower, butternut squash and kale into the cheese sauce and stir through gently.

Dust a work surface with flour and, using a rolling pin, roll out the pastry into a large rectangle 3–4mm thick. Cut into equal-sized squares – you can either make four large ones or eight small ones. Imagine the squares as two triangles and add a spoonful of the cheesy vegetables to one triangle. Repeat with all the pastry squares.

Brush the beaten egg along the edges of the squares before folding the plain triangle of pastry over the filling and pinching and crimping the edges together so there are no gaps. You can do this with your fingers by folding and tucking the edges or dipping a fork in some flour and gently pressing down. Poke a little hole in the top of each pasty and then brush with the beaten egg. Bake for 20–30 minutes until the pastry is golden brown and you can see some cheesy bubbles.

Allow to cool slightly before eating. They can be reheated in the oven at 160°C fan (180°C/350°F/Gas Mark 4) for 10 minutes.

Beetroot, feta + nigella seed scones

MAKES 9 SCONES

75g unsalted butter, softened, plus extra for greasing
1½ tsp nigella seeds
300g self-raising flour, plus extra for dusting
150g strong white bread flour
2 tsp baking powder
½ tsp salt
½ tsp freshly ground black pepper
200g feta cheese, crumbled*
2 cooked beetroot, grated with some of the excess juice squeezed out
2 eggs
about 175ml whole milk

*Or use whatever cheese you fancy or have to hand.

The natural colouring from beetroot is one of my absolute favourites. Nigella seeds give a little onion contrast to the cheese, but cumin or fennel seeds work well too. I think scones are the perfect companion to hot, thick soup, but are also great toasted and slathered in salted butter instead of boring old toast. They are so fast to make and in about half an hour you have delicious baked goodies and a home smelling like pure comfort.

Preheat the oven to 180°C fan (200°C/400°F/Gas Mark 6) and grease a large, flat baking tray.

Scatter the nigella seeds over the baking tray and pop into the oven for 5 minutes to toast briefly. Remove from the oven and set aside.

Sift the flours, baking powder, salt and pepper into a large bowl. Add the butter and rub in with your fingertips until the mixture resembles breadcrumbs. Stir in the cooled nigella seeds and stir through the crumbled feta with a blunt knife. Then add the grated beetroot and stir through with the same blunt knife, making sure everything is coated in the flour.

Lightly beat the eggs in a measuring jug, add the milk and stir. Make a well in the middle of the dry ingredients. Pour in about three quarters of the egg mixture and use a blunt knife to mix in. Add more egg mixture if needed – the mixture will be wetter due to the beetroot. There should be some egg mixture left to glaze the scones. Finish mixing with your hands, but be careful not to handle the dough too much.

Dust a work surface with flour and turn the dough out, using your hands to bring it together. Flatten the dough out until it is 5–7.5cm thick and shape into a large square. Cut into nine equal squares using a sharp knife. You can also use a cutter or cut into wedges. Space the scones out on the prepared baking tray and glaze with the remaining egg mixture.

Bake for 12–15 minutes until golden, risen and smelling delightful. Remove from the oven and transfer to a wire rack to cool. Serve warm with a smear of salted butter.

Courgette, chickpea + halloumi falafel

SERVES 4

1 courgette
225g halloumi
1 x 400g tin chickpeas, drained and rinsed
2 garlic cloves, roughly chopped
1 red chilli, roughly chopped
small bunch of fresh dill
few sprigs of fresh mint, leaves only
zest and juice of 1 lemon
½ tsp ground cumin
¼ tsp ground cinnamon
50g pine nuts
50g fresh breadcrumbs
oil, to fry
salt and freshly ground black pepper
pitta bread, salad, tzatziki (page 21) and chilli sauce, to serve (optional)

Shout out to *This Country* and Daisy May Cooper for this one as I can't make or see or say the word 'falafel' without shouting it! You need TV shows like this to lift your mood. I love falafel but they can be a little claggy sometimes, so I made these fragrant, moist little balls that fit snuggly in toasted pitta breads, nestle happily alongside couscous and hummus or can be popped straight in your gob!

Coarsely grate the courgette, squeeze out any excess water and place in a bowl.

Coarsely grate the halloumi and add this to the bowl with the courgette.

Put the chickpeas, garlic, chilli, dill, mint, lemon zest and juice in a food processor or blender and blitz until you have a coarse consistency. You do not want a purée so blitz in short blasts. Scrape the mixture into the bowl with the courgette and halloumi and mix together.

Sprinkle over the cumin, cinnamon, pine nuts and breadcrumbs and season with some salt and pepper. Get your hands in and give everything a really good squeeze and mix together – I find this is the best way of getting all the flavours evenly distributed. Transfer to the fridge for about 30 minutes to firm up.

Place a little oil on your hands to stop the mixture from sticking and shape your falafels. (If your falafel mixture is still a little wet, you can add some more breadcrumbs.) Now it's up to you if you want your falafels golf-ball sized, as flattened patties or burger-sized. Shape your falafels and place on a plate.

Heat a little oil in a pan over a medium heat and add the falafels. Fry for 2–3 minutes on each size for flattened patties and a little longer for balls. Finish cooking in the oven at 160°C fan (180°C/350°F/Gas Mark 4) for 10 minutes.

Serve with pitta bread, a heap of salad, tzatziki and chilli sauce, as you wish.

Bacon, cheese + chive croquettes

SERVES 4 WITH A GOOD PORTION EACH OR LOTS FOR A SHARER

2–3 potatoes, peeled and chopped into 2.5cm cubes (I used Maris piper)
large knob of butter
100ml double cream
6 rashers of smoked streaky bacon
4 spring onions
small bunch of fresh chives
150g Manchego cheese, grated
150g Cheddar cheese, grated
2 eggs
150g plain flour
200g fresh breadcrumbs made from blitzed up bread slices
2 litres vegetable oil
salt and freshly ground black pepper
chilli and red onion chutney, to serve (optional)

We needed a new starter for the pub, so these were born, and my goodness did they fly out of the kitchen. We literally couldn't keep up. They are not authentically Spanish but more just an experiment to see how much cheese and bacon we could fit into a bite-sized morsel and then deep fry it. Get the dips alongside and you've got yourself finger food at its best. You can swap bacon for fried mushrooms or spinach for a veggie version and also freeze before coating in the egg and breadcrumbs.

Bring a saucepan of salted water to the boil over a high heat and once it starts to boil, add the potatoes and cook for about 20 minutes until soft and easy to mash with a fork. Drain.

Add half the butter and the cream to the cooked potatoes and mash until the potatoes are smooth.

Set a frying pan over a medium heat, slice the bacon into small strips and add to the pan. Chop the spring onions and add to the hot frying pan along with the remaining butter. Fry until the bacon is crispy and the spring onions are soft. Tip into the mashed potato.

Finely chop the chives and add to the mash. Mix the grated cheeses together and then tip into the mashed potato. Mix together until well combined. You may want to do this with your hands. Taste a little and season with salt and pepper.

Shape the potato and bacon mixture into thumb-sized pieces shaped like little potato sausages. Set out on some greaseproof paper and transfer to the fridge to set for 30 minutes to 1 hour.

Continued overleaf →

Beat the eggs together in a small bowl and put the flour and breadcrumbs into two separate bowls.

Heat the vegetable oil in a deep-fat fryer or if using a large saucepan, make sure it's deep enough to hold at least 5cm oil in the bottom and heat the oil to about 190°C (375°F). You can test the heat of the oil by dropping in a cube of bread – if it sizzles, turns golden brown and floats to the top then it's ready.

Roll the chilled potato croquettes in the flour, then dip into the beaten egg and finally roll in the breadcrumbs until they are completely covered.

Fry off 4–5 croquettes at a time for 3–5 minutes until golden, turning halfway through cooking. You can keep warm or finish off in the oven at 140°C fan (160°C/325°F/Gas Mark 3) for up to 10 minutes while you finish batch frying the remaining croquettes.

Serve hot and gooey with chilli and red onion chutney.

My type of pizza

MAKES 6

500ml warm water
10g instant yeast
900g '00' flour
10g caster sugar
12g fine sea salt
6 tbsp olive oil, plus extra
   for brushing and drizzling
semolina, for dusting

TOPPING:
200g very soft unsalted butter
4 garlic cloves
100g kale, stripped from the
   tough stalks
10 string cheeses, each split
   into 4 pieces
6 large mushrooms, finely
   sliced (I used large
   Portobello)
200g black olives, roughly
   chopped
15–18 slices of prosciutto
3 x 125g balls of mozzarella,
   very well drained, or pizza
   mozzarella
sea salt and black pepper
Grana Padano, to serve

This is how I have my pizza. You may notice here and in my first book the lack of tomato sauce as I'm not a huge fan of it, especially on pizza. If I'm having a takeaway or restaurant pizza, I always ask for a garlic butter base instead. So here is my fully loaded garlic bread pizza. You may notice my other guilty pleasure in there – string cheese for the stuffed crust win! (Yes I am a child, yes I always have these in my fridge.) You can add whatever toppings you like – this is just my favourite combo.

Pour the warm water into a jug, mix in the yeast and leave for 8–10 minutes until it starts to bubble and foam.

Sift the flour into the bowl of a free-standing electric mixer fitted with a dough hook and make a well in the middle. Place the sugar and salt on one side and start mixing on low speed. Pour in 450ml of the yeasty water and the olive oil and mix until all of the flour has been incorporated. If the dough is too dry, add a little more of the yeasty water. If you don't have a mixer, you can use your hands to bring the mixture together.

If using a free-standing electric mixer, set to a medium speed and mix for 7–8 minutes until the dough is smooth and elastic. If kneading by hand, then knead for about 10 minutes.

Tip the dough on to a lightly oiled surface and using a sharp knife, cut the dough into six equal pieces and then roll these into six balls. Lightly grease a baking sheet and space the dough balls out on the sheet. Using olive oil, oil the top of each piece of dough and lightly cover with clingfilm. Place somewhere warm for 1–2 hours or until at least doubled in size.

To make the garlic kale butter, place the butter, garlic, kale leaves and some salt and pepper in a food processor and blitz until smooth and combined with flecks of lovely green kale.

Preheat the oven to 220°C fan (240°C/475°F/Gas Mark 9). If you have a pizza or bread stone, put this in the oven.

Once the dough has risen, remove a ball from the sheet and knock the air out with your knuckles. Use your fingertips or the heel of your hand to spread the dough into a circle. You can lift it gently and use its own weight to stretch it further until you have a circle about 30–35cm in diameter (depending how thick you want the base of your pizza). Repeat with the remaining balls of dough.

Sprinkle a good amount of semolina on a pizza tray or flat baking sheet, or on the pre-warmed pizza stone. Spread some of the garlic kale butter all over the pizza bases, leaving about a 2.5cm border clear around the edges.

Lay pieces of string cheese around the edge of the pizza base, fold over the edges of the dough and tuck under, encasing the string cheese completely (stuffed crust, y'all!).

Scatter some sliced mushrooms and chopped olives over the pizza base. Top with torn prosciutto and tear up the mozzarella and scatter over. Drizzle with olive oil. Bake for 12–15 minutes until the cheese is bubbling and the dough is golden and crisp underneath. Remove from the oven and grate over a little Grana Padano, wait a minute or two, then slice and eat. You might not want to kiss anyone after this!

Use something that's easy to transfer into the oven once the toppings are on.

Salmon + edamame bean fishcakes

**MAKES 2 LARGER OR
4 SMALLER FISHCAKES**

2 salmon fillets, skin on
½ lemon, sliced
200g edamame beans
   (frozen then defrosted)
8 tbsp mashed potatoes,
   cooled
½ tsp chilli flakes
4 spring onions, chopped
small bunch of fresh flat-leaf
   parsley, finely chopped
4 heaped tsp garlic and herb
   cream cheese
1 egg, beaten
2 slices of stale bread or 75g
   ready-made breadcrumbs
1 heaped tsp plain flour
1 tsp dried parsley
olive oil
salt and freshly ground
   black pepper

I love fishcakes, but got so fed up with having fishcakes that were made with mainly potato or with peas (you know how I feel about peas!). So, I had a play with some beautiful just-cooked salmon and edamame beans and came up with these. There's still potato in there, but it's joined by some creamy cheese in the middle. Smoked haddock works well in these too – just mind the seasoning – and try smoked mackerel for something a little different.

Preheat the oven to 160°C fan (180°C/350°F/Gas Mark 4).

Put the salmon fillets on a piece of foil and lay the lemon slices over the top. Roll the edges of the foil up to create a little parcel with no gaps, but leave some air to circulate. Transfer to a baking tray and cook for 15–18 minutes. Set aside to cool.

Put the edamame beans in a large bowl and cover with boiling water. Leave to blanch for 5 minutes. Drain.

Put the blanched beans and mashed potatoes in a large bowl, sprinkle over the chilli flakes and add the spring onions and parsley. Season with salt and pepper and give it a good mix with your hands.

Remove the skin from the salmon and discard along with the lemon slices. Flake the salmon into the potato mixture and gently mix together, trying not to break the fish up too much.

Continued overleaf →

Use your hands to make four equal patties and flatten them out. Add a heaped teaspoon of the cream cheese to the middle of each fish patty and then gently bring up the edges and encase the cream cheese in the fish mixture, making sure there are no gaps. Flatten down into nice little fishcakes.

If using slices of bread, blitz the bread in a food processor with the flour and dried parsley to make breadcrumbs, then tip on to a plate. If using ready-made breadcrumbs, pop them on to a plate and mix in the flour and dried parsley.

Brush the fishcakes with the beaten egg, then press them into the breadcrumbs, gently rolling to coat the fishcakes completely. Place on a plate and transfer to the fridge to chill for 20–30 minutes.

Lightly oil a baking tray and place the fishcakes on the tray. Cook for 25–30 minutes until golden brown.

Just wait for that ooze when you cut in...

Homemade gnocchi

Perfect for the Pesto Gnocchi Gratin on page 67!

SERVES 4
(makes enough for the gratin on page 67)

400g fluffy potatoes, peeled
2 egg yolks, beaten
1 tsp dried basil
200g '00' flour
salt and pepper

Carb on carb and pure comfort! I was taught to make these by our chef, even though I had to ask him about a hundred times for the quantities as my brain couldn't retain the numbers. It's so simple but so much better than shop-bought and can be frozen too. Serve simply with a huge knob of salted butter, a good grind of black pepper and some torn sage, grated Parmesan and good olive oil or stir through some pesto or even a couple of tablespoons of a hot chunky mushroom soup as a cheat sauce.

Preheat the oven to 160°C fan (180°C/350°F/Gas Mark 4).

Give the potatoes a little wash and pierce the skins with a sharp knife. Place on a baking tray and bake for 1–1½ hours until soft when gently squeezed. You can speed this process up by piercing the skin of the potatoes and putting them in the microwave for 4–5 minutes and then in the oven for 30–45 minutes. Remove from the oven and allow to cool fully.

Once cool enough to handle, slice the potatoes in half and scoop out all the soft middle and either pass through a potato ricer into a large bowl or put in a bowl and use a masher to really mash the hell out of them. Make a well in the centre and pour in the egg, then add a pinch of salt and pepper and the dried basil. Mix together until you have an eggy potato dough.

Place the flour on a work surface and then dump the potato dough on top. Start to knead the flour into the potato until you have a smooth yet workable, non-sticky dough. (You may not need all the flour.)

Divide the dough in two and roll into two long sausages about 2.5cm in diameter. Chop into gnocchi-sized pieces. You can also freeze the gnocchi in this long sausage form and slice to defrost when needed.

If you want to be fancy you can roll your gnocchi off a fork to make little grooves or leave them as they are.

To cook, place in a saucepan of salted boiling water and remove with a slotted spoon as soon as they start to float – this can take as little as 1–2 minutes. Drain immediately.

White chocolate, cardamom, almond + lemon pastry twists

MAKES 15–20

150g plain flour, plus extra
    for dusting
150g strong white bread flour
4 cardamom pods, seeds
    removed and crushed
zest of 1 lemon
pinch of salt
50g lard, cubed
150ml cold water
200g unsalted butter, chilled
25g very soft butter
150g white chocolate, grated
50g ground almonds
100g flaked almonds
1 egg beaten, for egg wash

The ultimate take-your-time bake, simply because you are going to make puff pastry from scratch. It's a long process, but so worth it because the satisfaction of knowing you have made the flakiest, most buttery pastry that you then lovingly twist and fill with chocolate is a great feeling. Sometimes you need a little sense of achievement to feel better and that's OK. These do it for me – I hope they can for you too. Undercook them slightly if you're like me and like a little stodge.

Sift both types of flour into a large bowl and stir in the crushed cardamom, lemon zest and salt. Add the lard and rub in with your fingertips until the mixture resembles breadcrumbs. Stir in the cold water and bring together with your hands to make a dough.

Turn the dough out on to a lightly floured work surface and knead briefly until smooth. Wrap in clingfilm and transfer to the fridge to chill for at least 30 minutes.

Remove the dough from the fridge on to a floured work surface and roll away from you to form a rectangle about 20 x 40cm.

Place the chilled butter between two pieces of greaseproof paper and bash and roll with a rolling pin to make a 15 x 25cm rectangle that is about 3mm thick. Great for thrashing out any anger! Lay the butter rectangle on the bottom two-thirds of the dough – there should be about a 1cm clear border at the sides and bottom. Fold the top third (without butter) down over the middle third, then fold the bottom third up over the middle third (you will now have alternating layers of dough, butter, dough, butter, dough). Pinch the edges together, wrap in clingfilm and chill for 30 minutes.

Remove the dough from the fridge and place on a floured work surface so a short side is facing you. Roll out away from you to form a 20 x 40cm rectangle again. This time fold both the top and bottom of the rectangle in so they meet in the middle, then fold over in half like a book. Pinch the edges together. Chill for 30 minutes.

Place the dough on a floured work surface so a short side is facing you and roll out away from you to form a 20 x 40cm rectangle again. Fold the top third down over the middle third, then fold the bottom third up over this. Wrap and chill for 30 minutes. Repeat this rolling and folding three more times with a 30-minute chilling in between each one.

Cut the pastry in half. You need just one half for the straws. The other half can be wrapped in clingfilm and kept in the fridge for five days or in the freezer for up to one month.

Roll the pastry into a rectangle about 3mm thick. Spread the soft butter on the middle third of the pastry, then sprinkle over half the white chocolate and ground almonds, then fold the top third down on top of it. Spread more butter over the top, sprinkle over the remaining chocolate and ground almonds, then fold the bottom third up over the top. Pinch the edges together and gently roll to flatten slightly. Wrap in clingfilm and chill for 30 minutes.

Preheat the oven to 200°C fan (220°C/425°F/Gas Mark 7) and line two baking sheets with greaseproof paper.

Roll out the dough to a large rectangle about 4mm thick and cut into 15–20 strips measuring 2.5cm wide. Lift each strip and gently twist it a couple of times so you have a spiral, then place on the baking sheets. Gently push the top and bottom of each strip on to the sheet so it doesn't unravel. Brush the twists with the beaten egg. Sprinkle with the flaked almonds and bake for about 20 minutes until golden and crisp.

The twists will keep in an airtight container for two days and can be freshened up in the oven at 160°C fan (180°C/350°F/Gas Mark 4) for 5 minutes.

Rocky road cookies

**MAKES 8–10 LARGE
OR 12–15 SMALL**

125g unsalted butter, softened
200g golden caster sugar
1 large egg
160g plain flour
25g cocoa powder
½ tsp baking powder
pinch of salt
75g dried cherries, halved
75g pistachios, chopped
50g mini marshmallows
7 speculoos biscuits, broken
   into pieces (I used Biscoff)
100g white chocolate,
   chopped into chunks
100g crunchy speculoos
   biscuit spread (I used
   Biscoff) or peanut butter

You've heard of rocky road, so now take your rocky road and put it in a soft, chewy cookie and you get these delights. They are unbelievably indulgent, but sometimes we just need that treat that makes us sit back, breathe a huge sigh of relief and say 'oh, I needed that!' These are great for using up biscuits and little sweets – you can also pop a little something in the middle for an extra surprise.

Preheat the oven to 160°C fan (180°C/350°F/Gas Mark 4) and line two large baking sheets with greaseproof paper.

Put the butter and sugar in a large mixing bowl and cream together until fluffy using an electric mixer – this will take a few minutes. Add the egg and mix well. If the mixture starts to curdle, add a spoonful of the flour. Sift the flour, cocoa, baking powder and salt into the bowl and mix until combined.

Add the cherries, pistachios and mini marshmallows, then fold through the biscuits and chocolate.

Drop heaped dessertspoons of the mixture on to the prepared baking sheets, then slightly dent the middle of each one with your finger before adding ½ teaspoon of speculoos biscuit spread or peanut butter. Cover with a little more cookie dough and seal the edges with a finger so the speculoos spread or peanut butter is completely enclosed. Shape each one into a ball slightly larger than a golf ball.

Bake for 10–12 minutes (10 minutes for super-gooey cookies, 12 minutes for firmer). Leave to cool on the baking sheets for a couple of minutes before carefully moving to a wire rack to cool completely.

These keep in an airtight container for two days – they won't last two days though, trust me.

Apricot + almond decorated biscuits

MAKES 15–20 BISCUITS
(depending on the size of the
cutters)

85g golden caster sugar
170g unsalted butter, softened
250g plain flour, plus extra for
dusting
25g ground almonds
pinch of salt
75g almonds, chopped
75g dried apricots, chopped
25ml amaretto
200g icing sugar
gel food colouring of your
choice
sprinkles, melted chocolate
and/or edible dried flowers,
to decorate (optional)

*These are lovely
un-iced and with
various other dried
fruit too.*

I don't think I'm the best decorator, so it can be quite detrimental for me to sit and do something like this as I don't ever think it will be good enough. But sometimes it's more about the process and just sitting, taking time and enjoying what you are doing.

Put the sugar in a bowl, then add the butter and mix until well combined. Add the flour, ground almonds and salt and mix through. Add the chopped almonds, dried apricots and amaretto and mix in with your hands until combined – do not over work the dough. Remove the dough from the bowl, flatten and wrap in clingfilm. Transfer to the fridge to chill for 30 minutes.

Preheat the oven to 160°C fan (180°C/350°F/Gas Mark 4) and line a baking tray with greaseproof paper.

Lightly flour a work surface and roll out the dough until 4–5mm thick. Cut out the biscuits using whatever shaped cutters you fancy – I like using hearts and stars. Bring the cuttings back together, re-roll and continue to cut out until you have used up all the dough and have 15–20 biscuits (depending on the size of your cutters).

Place the biscuits on to the prepared tray with space in between each one and chill in the fridge for 15 minutes.

Remove the biscuits from the fridge and bake for 15–20 minutes until golden brown. Gently lift the biscuits on to a wire rack to cool. You can eat them warm without decorating at this stage if you wish.

Mix the icing sugar with some water until you have a smooth, thick paste. Divide the icing into bowls and mix with a few drops of food colouring gel so you have the colour(s) of your choice. I used white and dried flowers to decorate mine. Transfer the icing to piping bags and snip a small hole at the ends. Decorate the biscuits however you like. You can also go nuts with sprinkles, melted chocolate and/or edible dried flowers, if you like. Leave to set and dry.

These will keep in an airtight biscuit tin for 3–4 days.

Image overleaf →

Honey + lemon round challah

SERVES 6-8

500g strong white bread flour
7g instant yeast
7g fine sea salt
1 tsp ground ginger
1 tsp freshly grated ginger
zest of 1 lemon
50g honey
200ml lukewarm water
   (you may need a little more)
3 eggs, 1 beaten with a
   little water
50ml light olive oil,
   plus extra for greasing

Kneading and knocking the air out of dough is the ultimate therapy for me. When I need something to do with my hands, or I need to take some frustration out, bread is what I go to, which is why I have given two options for kneading – with a machine or by hand if you need that knead. Braiding is not that difficult when you know how, trying to explain it on the other hand is the hard part. Watch a video and follow the hands and you'll find it so much easier. If you want a plain challah, leave out the lemon and ginger or substitute them for other citrus zests or ground cinnamon.

Put the flour in the bowl of a free-standing electric mixer fitted with the dough hook and make a well in the middle. Add the yeast to one side of the well and the salt, ground and fresh ginger and lemon zest to the opposite side.

Mix the honey with the warm water in a jug.

Crack two eggs into the well, add the oil, then start the mixer on a low speed and slowly pour the honey water in. You want a soft but not wet dough, so go slow with the water. Once all the flour has been incorporated, turn the mixer up to medium and knead for 6–7 minutes until you have a soft, stretchy and beautifully fragranced dough. If kneading by hand, bring all the ingredients together with your hands, then turn out on to a work surface and knead for 10–12 minutes.

Lightly grease a large bowl and place the dough inside. Grease a piece of clingfilm and lay this over the top of the bowl, then set aside in a warm place for 1 hour 30 minutes to 2 hours or until at least doubled in size.

Once the dough has risen, use your knuckles to knock the air out and turn out on to a lightly greased work surface. Divide into four equal pieces and roll into sausages about 65cm in length. If the dough keeps pinging back, then cover lightly with a damp tea towel and leave for a couple of minutes.

Take two strands of dough and lay them next to each other horizontally. Then lay the remaining two strands across the top, slightly apart, to form a cross. Weave one vertical strand over and under the two (horizontal) strands underneath, then do the opposite with the strand next to it (so weave it under and over). Starting at the top of the cross and working clockwise, take a strand that's underneath and move it over its neighbouring strand. Repeat with the next strand along, then with the third and finally with the fourth. Now go back in the opposite (anticlockwise) direction with the strands underneath, moving them along and over the top of their neighbouring strand. The underneath strand always goes over the top of the strand next to it. Continue until you have braided all the strands, then tuck the ends right under and shape the challah gently so you have a round, almost upside-down weaved basket.

Place your braided challah on a baking tray lined with greaseproof paper and put this into a large plastic bag (filled with air). Set aside in a warm place for 45 minutes to 1 hour until the dough has risen and springs back when poked.

Preheat oven to 180°C fan (200°C/400°F/Gas Mark 6).

Gently glaze the dough with the beaten egg using a pastry brush. Bake the challah for 30–40 minutes until golden and risen. The bread is cooked when it sounds hollow when tapped on the bottom. If it starts to brown too quickly, then reduce the temperature by 10–20°C for the last 10 minutes of cooking or loosely cover with foil.

Remove from the oven and place on a wire rack to cool. Serve warm.

It's also great toasted with butter the next day.

Swedish cinnamon buns (Kanelbullar)

MAKES 15–20

250ml whole milk
10 cardamom pods, broken open
70g light soft brown sugar, plus 1 tbsp
7g instant yeast
450g plain flour, plus extra for dusting
1 tsp salt
zest of 1 lemon
1 tsp ground cinnamon
2 eggs, 1 beaten with a dash of water and pinch of salt
80g very soft unsalted butter
olive oil
maple syrup, to drizzle
50g flaked almonds, toasted

FILLING:
80g unsalted butter, softened
70g light soft brown sugar
25g ground almonds
4 tsp ground cinnamon
1 tsp ground cardamom (about 8 pods)
1 tsp ground ginger
½ tsp freshly grated nutmeg

I went to West Sweden a couple of years ago and loved everything about it, not just their fondness for cinnamon buns and coffee, but their way of life and *fika* – taking time out of every day to sit down with a Kanelbullar or cake and coffee and another person to converse, listen and interact with each other. Life moves so fast that we sometimes forget to do this, eating at desks, grabbing coffee on the move, stuck to our phones. Let's talk more, face to face, ask how someone is and take the time to breathe and enjoy that cinnamon bun.

Put the milk, cardamom pods and 1 tablespoon of brown sugar in a small saucepan and heat until blood temperature – if you dip your finger in, you shouldn't be able to feel it as the liquid is the same temperature as your blood. Mix in the yeast and set aside for about 10 minutes until the yeast has frothed and foamed on top of the milk.

Mix the flour, sugar, salt, lemon zest and cinnamon together in the bowl of a free-standing electric mixer fitted with the dough hook, then create a well in the middle. Add the egg to the well. Set on low-medium speed and as the egg starts to mix through, slowly add the warm frothy milk (remove the cardamom pods prior to pouring and any seeds that may have escaped) and mix until combined. Knead for 2–3 minutes on low-medium speed until everything has come together. Now add the very soft butter a little at a time until completely incorporated. Knead for 7–8 minutes until the dough is smooth and stretchy. It should stretch so you can see light through it, but not break. If you don't have a free-standing electric mixer, you can do the kneading by hand which will take about 10–12 minutes and be a great stress relief.

Grease a large bowl with a little oil, place the dough in and cover with greased clingfilm. Leave in a warm place for about two hours or until the dough has at least doubled in size.

Continued overleaf →

Once the dough has proved, knock the air out of it with your knuckles before tipping it out on to a lightly oiled work surface and folding it over on itself a couple of times. Roll the dough into a 30 x 20cm rectangle – if the dough keeps springing back, then cover with a tea towel and leave for 5 minutes.

In a large bowl, whip together all the filling ingredients until soft and spreadable using a wooden spoon or handheld electric mixer. Spread the spiced butter all over the dough rectangle. Then, with the short end facing you, fold one third of the dough into the middle, then fold the remaining end over the top, as if you were folding a piece of paper to fit in an envelope. Chill in the fridge for 20 minutes for the filling to firm up.

Remove from the fridge and place on a lightly floured work surface. Roll the dough into a rectangle about 50 x 20cm, keeping it as straight as possible. From the short end, cut into strips 2.5cm wide all the way along – you should get about 15–20 strips.

Try not to roll from the middle or you will squash the filling out.

Hold one end of a strip on the work surface, then twist the strip several times (think cheese twist). Then hold one end of the twist between your thumb and middle finger and with the opposite end in your other hand, circle the strip once round the thumb, first finger and middle finger in a clockwise motion, slightly parting your fingers to tuck the end in through the middle like a knot.

Place the bun on a baking tray lined with greaseproof paper – you will need two baking trays for all the buns. Repeat with all the strips of dough, leaving space between each bun. Place the trays into large bags or loosely cover with greased clingfilm and leave in a warm place for about 1 hour until the dough has risen and springs back when poked.

Preheat the oven to 175°C fan (195°C/400°F/Gas Mark 6).

Brush each bun with the beaten egg mixture, then bake for 20–25 minutes until the buns are golden and risen.

Remove from the oven and transfer to a wire rack. Drizzle over the maple syrup, sprinkle with toasted flaked almonds and serve warm. These will keep overnight stored in an airtight container and can be freshened up in the oven at 160°C fan (180°C/350°F/Gas Mark 4) for 10 minutes.

Apricot + amaretto pastel de nata

MAKES 12

375g roll or block of puff
  pastry, chilled
6 apricots
handful of flaked almonds
2 tsp demerara sugar

CUSTARD:
250ml whole milk
250ml double cream
1 tbsp amaretto
30g golden caster sugar
pinch of salt
2 egg yolks
20g cornflour

You can finish off the tarts with a kitchen blowtorch if you want a deeper colour.

Dreamy, smooth amaretto custard and a big juicy apricot nestled in crisp, swirled pastry. I'll have two please. I love how these tarts kind of go against the grain of normal pastry because you roll, flatten and swirl. A bit like my brain, I think. It's OK to be different, different is good and tasty. Raspberries work well instead of the apricots as does rhubarb when it's in season.

To make the custard, put the milk, cream and amaretto in a medium saucepan over a low-medium heat and stir until just bubbling.

Mix the sugar, salt, egg yolks and cornflour together in a bowl to make a smooth paste. Pour in a small amount of the hot milk and cream and stir through. Add a little more and mix, then continuously pour in the rest of the hot milk, stirring constantly.

Rinse and dry the saucepan, then pour the mixture back in. Set over a low heat and stir constantly until the custard is thick and smooth. Set aside.

Allow the pastry to come to room temperature, then either roll out into a rectangle about 40 x 50cm and 3mm thick or unroll the pre-rolled pastry. With a short side facing you, tightly roll the pastry back up into a roll. Slice the roll into 2–2.5cm-wide discs.

Preheat the oven to 160°C fan (180°C/350°F/Gas Mark 4).

Place a disc of pastry into the bottom of each hole of a greased 12-hole muffin or bun tin and, using your thumb, smooth up the edges of the pastry, starting from the middle until it slightly overlaps the rim of the hole. Pour the custard into each pastry case until three quarters full. Slice the apricots in half and remove the stone. Place half an apricot, hole-side up, on top of each tart. Scatter each tart with some flaked almonds and demerara sugar. Bake for 20–25 minutes until the pastry is golden and the custard is starting to turn a deep golden brown.

Remove from the oven and carefully place each tart on to a wire rack to cool. Keep in a container in the fridge for two days and reheat in the oven 160°C fan (180°C/350°F/Gas Mark 4) for 10 minutes.

Chocolate caramel babka

SERVES 6-8

100ml whole milk

2 tbsp honey

7g instant yeast

250g strong white bread flour

7g fine sea salt

2 tsp ground cinnamon

1 egg

100ml coconut oil, softened, plus extra for greasing

50g dark chocolate (minimum 70% cocoa solids), coarsely grated

50g caramel sauce (homemade or use Carnation caramel), plus extra to serve

50g toasted hazelnuts, chopped

½ tsp sea salt flakes

1 egg, beaten with a dash of water and pinch of salt

50g light soft brown sugar

I just like saying the word 'babka' if I'm honest. I also like eating this. Another wonderful sweet bread that makes good use of your hands when the fidgets get too much. I make most of my bread when my ADHD gets too much. It keeps me busy and I know what I'm getting out of it! You can put most things in a babka, but you just need to be aware of a runny or softer filling that makes the dough wetter as this can mean you'll need to leave it to rise and bake for a little longer. The coconut oil gives a lovely light texture and keeps your hands soft too.

Heat the milk and honey in a small saucepan until blood temperature – if you dip your finger in, you shouldn't be able to feel it as the liquid is the same temperature as your blood. Mix in the yeast and set aside for 10 minutes until the yeast has frothed and foamed on top of the milk.

Mix the flour, salt and half the cinnamon together in the large bowl of a free-standing electric mixer fitted with the dough hook, then create a well in the middle. Add the egg to the well. Set on low speed and add the warm frothy milk as it starts to knead. Knead the dough for 2 minutes on low-medium speed until all the flour is incorporated, then add the coconut oil in three stages, mixing in between each one. Knead for 5–7 minutes until the dough is smooth and stretchy. If you don't have a mixer, then you can do all the kneading by hand for 10–12 minutes.

Grease a large bowl with a little coconut oil, add the dough and cover with greased clingfilm. Leave in a warm place for 1–2 hours or until the dough has at least doubled in size.

Lightly oil a work surface and tip the dough out. Use your knuckles to knock the air out of the dough and your palms to spread it out. Roll it into a rectangle about 25 x 40cm – if the dough keeps springing back, cover it with a tea towel and leave for 5 minutes.

Continued overleaf →

Spread the chocolate all over the dough, drizzle over the caramel sauce and sprinkle over the hazelnuts and sea salt. From one long end, tightly roll the dough into a long Swiss roll. Put the join underneath and, with a sharp knife, slice the Swiss roll lengthways all the way along keeping about 4cm at one end joined. Twist the two halves around each other and place in a greased and lined 900g loaf tin. It may need to double over on itself, so slightly zigzag it over itself if so. Place the tin in a large plastic bag and leave the dough to rise in a warm place for about 45 minutes until about doubled in size.

Preheat the oven to 160°C fan (180°C/350°F/Gas Mark 4).

Glaze the risen babka with the beaten egg mixture. Mix together the remaining 1 teaspoon of cinnamon and the brown sugar and sprinkle over the top. Bake for 40–50 minutes until it is golden, risen and sounds hollow when tapped on the bottom.

Leave to cool in the tin for 10 minutes, then transfer to a wire rack. Serve in warm slices drizzled with caramel. It is even better the next day toasted with salted butter and will keep in an airtight container for two days, but will need warming or toasting after the first.

Or you can prove the babka overnight in the fridge and then allow it to come to room temperature before baking.

Apple + pear sweet 'dauphinoise'

SERVES 6–8

250ml double cream
300ml whole milk
1 egg
50g light soft brown sugar
30g cornflour
pinch of salt
zest 1 orange
½ tsp ground cinnamon
large knob of butter
3 cooking apples, such as
   Bramley, peeled
3 Conference pears, peeled
25g demerara sugar
3 shortbread biscuits
80g pistachios

You want the ultimate head jumble? Then this dish messes with your senses. It looks just like its potato-ey sibling, but it's SWEET! Tangy apples and juicy pear slices cooked in custard and topped with crunchy nuts. No creamy onion here, just something a little different and a real talking point. Want to while away some time and keep those hands busy, then arrange the slices in perfect uniform layers or even vertically for a little difference. Give this one time to set once cooked as you want slices for maximum impact.

Preheat the oven to 160°C fan (180°C/350°F/Gas Mark 4).

Heat the double cream and milk in a saucepan over a medium heat until simmering and bubbles break the surface.

Whisk the egg, sugar, cornflour, salt, orange zest and cinnamon together in a large bowl until the mixture thickens and pales slightly. Pour the hot milk and cream into the bowl in a careful and steady stream, whisking constantly until combined. Pour the combined mixture back into the saucepan and put back over a low heat. Stir constantly until the custard thickens slightly and the cornflour has cooked out. Remove from the heat, drop in the butter and stir through.

If you are fancy and own a corer, remove the cores from the peeled apples and pears, then slice into rings 4–5mm thick. If you don't have a corer, then slice the apples and pears into quarters, cut out the cores, then slice lengthways.

Continued overleaf →

Line a 25cm round or square pie dish with greaseproof paper, place on a baking tray and layer in the apples and pears, making sure there are no gaps. Pour over the custard and give it a jiggle around. Sprinkle over the demerara sugar and bake for 45–50 minutes until the top is golden and the custard has set.

Remove from the oven and set aside to cool. Then place in the fridge for 3–4 hours to really firm up.

Crush the shortbread biscuits and roughly chop the pistachios and mix together.

Once the 'dauphinoise' has cooled completely, slice into wedges or squares and either heat up and serve warm with the shortbread and pistachio mix sprinkled over the top or serve cold in the same way.

It's a bit of a mind muddle as it looks so much like potato!

Gingerbread house

There's enough gingerbread here to feed a small village, but it'll do for 4–6 people over a couple of days!

700g plain flour
3 tsp ground cinnamon
3 tsp ground ginger
½ tsp freshly grated nutmeg
½ tsp salt
450g unsalted butter
700g dark soft brown sugar
2 large eggs
100g stem ginger in syrup, finely chopped
1 x bag of coloured boiled sweets (you need about 6–10 for the windows, but you might want some to eat while getting creative)
200g caster sugar

This should really give me heart palpitations and flashbacks to *The Great British Bake Off,* but actually it's something I can do quite well and brings back the most incredible memories. This isn't quite a pub but a cute little house that isn't just for Christmas but can be a task for you, for kids, or a gift for someone to put together themselves. The gingerbread is mighty tasty, so I suggest putting it together, taking a photo, then smashing it to pieces and eating the lot with a mug of my Hot chocolate orange (see page 45).

Preheat the oven to 160°C fan (180°C/350°F/Gas Mark 4) and line a baking tray with greaseproof paper.

Sift the flour, spices and salt into a bowl.

Put the butter and sugar in the bowl of free-standing electric mixer and mix until fluffy and light. You can also use a handheld electric mixer or even just a good old-fashioned wooden spoon and elbow grease. Add the eggs (and a little flour mix if it starts to curdle). Add the dry ingredients and the stem ginger and mix until just coming together.

Use your hands to form the dough into a ball, collecting all the dough from the edges of the bowl. Flatten, wrap in clingfilm and transfer to the fridge to chill for 30 minutes.

Roll out the dough between two sheets of greaseproof paper until 5–6mm thick. Using the templates on pages 130–31, cut out two sections for the front and back of the house, two side walls and two sections for the roof. You can also cut out a couple of people and some trees, if you wish, using a steady hand or cutters. Transfer to the prepared baking tray, then cut out the windows and door from the front and back sections following the templates. Place in the fridge for 30–45 minutes.

Remove from the fridge and bake for 10–15 minutes depending on size of the section. About halfway through baking (after 8 minutes), place a coloured boiled sweet in each empty window/door space.

Remove from the oven and very quickly, while hot and still soft, neaten the edges using a sharp knife and checking against the templates. Be careful of the melted sugar windows. Leave to cool slightly, then carefully transfer to a wire rack to cool completely.

DECORATION:

200g dark chocolate
(minimum 70% cocoa solids)
300g icing sugar
food colouring gels of
your choice
selection of sweets, such
as jelly sweets, milk and
white chocolate buttons,
sugar-coated chocolates
and/or jelly beans
a selection of nuts, such as
almonds and hazelnuts
desiccated coconut

Image on pages 132–33

To make the caramel for sticking, put the caster sugar and 50ml water in a saucepan over a medium heat. Swirl and allow the sugar to dissolve – do not mix, just swirl occasionally. Place a jam or cooking thermometer in the caramel and watch until the temperature reaches 160°C (325°F) – just past the hard crack stage. Swirl it around so it is an even colour and remove from the heat.

Before dipping in caramel, check the house sides fit together. If not, using a very sharp knife, simply shave off any excess until the sides fit.

Find a display board or surface on which you are going to display your house on and, working fast, dip the edges of the walls that are being joined in the caramel, one at time. Hold the walls together until the caramel hardens and the walls are stuck together. You may need some tins or something heavy to hold each section up while you do this and the caramel sets. If the caramel starts to harden, place briefly back over a low heat until it softens again.

Using a pastry brush, brush one side and one long edge of one roof piece (where it joins the other roof piece) with the caramel and hold on top of the walls. Repeat with the second roof piece and leave to set and harden. If you are not confident using hot caramel to stick, you can make up a thick paste using a little icing sugar and water and use this instead.

Melt the dark chocolate either in a bain-marie or in 20-second bursts in the microwave. Using a pastry brush, gently brush the melted chocolate on the roof so you get a thatched roof effect.

Put any remaining dark chocolate in a piping bag and use this to outline the windows or pipe on details.

In a bowl, mix the icing sugar together with some water and any food colouring you like to make a thick, pipeable paste. Transfer to a piping bag and use to decorate – use plain white icing for a snow effect around the roof and windows.

You can use sweets, nuts and/or coconut for decoration. Basically, go nuts! Decorate the house, trees and people, if using, and leave to set. If you're feeling fancy, you can put a small light under the house so the light shines through the coloured windows.

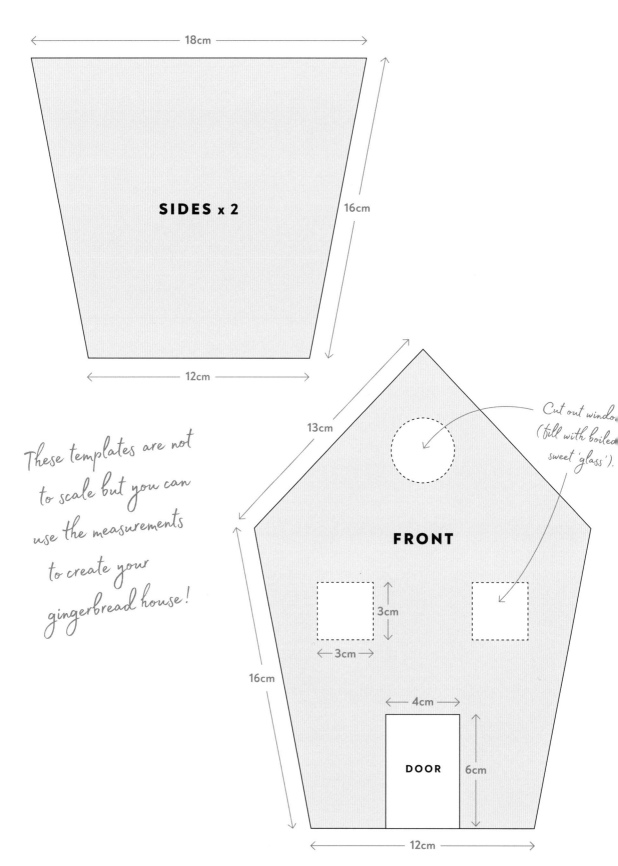

18cm

SIDES x 2

16cm

12cm

These templates are not to scale but you can use the measurements to create your gingerbread house!

13cm

Cut out window (fill with boiled sweet 'glass').

FRONT

3cm

3cm

16cm

4cm

DOOR

6cm

12cm

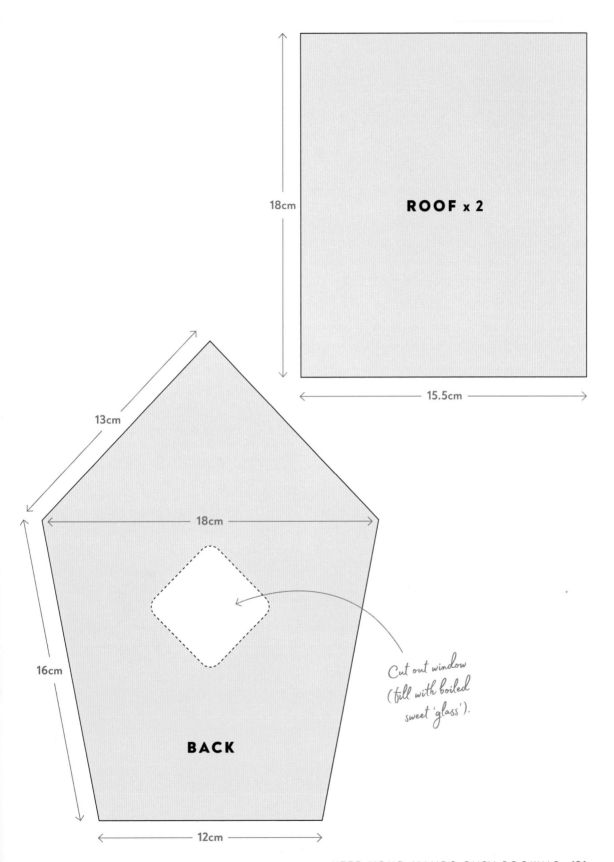

ROOF x 2

18cm

15.5cm

13cm

18cm

16cm

12cm

BACK

Cut out window
(fill with boiled
sweet 'glass').

Food that takes care of itself (and you)

SAVOURY:

Turmeric chicken and potatoes – 136

Leftover turmeric chicken, pearl barley
and mushroom soup – 138

Smoky bean chilli – 139

Slow-cooked beef brisket in ale – 140

Lamb, quinoa and feta – 145

Slow-cooked pork, celeriac and apple – 147

Mushroom, spinach and sweetcorn risotto – 148

Leek and potato soup with Stilton croutons – 149

Coconut, spinach and pistachio chana dhal – 153

SWEET:

Overnight porridge with apple, seeds and
goji berries – 154

Stewed fruit – 155

Chocolate, caramel and chia seed
rice pudding – 156

THROWING EVERYTHING into a slow cooker or a pot and just leaving it to cook and stew all day brings a certain kind of joy to me. This is the comforting, warming type of food that gives you a big cuddle without you really having to think much about it. Just whack it in and leave it to do its thing.

Slow-cooked food is all about flavour, but with minimum effort. Slow cookers are so versatile nowadays that they can be used overnight if you want something ready in the morning, or while you are at work or just first thing in the morning when you don't want to think about dinner later on. Done and dusted and tasty too – just get a bowl and spoon (most of these dishes can be eaten with a spoon because I find bowl-and-spoon food very comforting). Good for picky eaters too as slow cooking means vegetables are soft and take on other flavours so you are adding to your five-a-day without even realising it!

These recipes are perfect for when you want something hearty to come home to after a hard day. Find some of my favourite flavours in this chapter and also how to use up leftovers the next day. Two dishes for the effort of one! If you don't have a slow cooker, then you can pop it all in a covered ovenproof pot and leave in the oven or on the hob on a low setting instead.

Turmeric chicken + potatoes

SERVES 4

1.5–2kg whole chicken

3–4 potatoes, peeled and
  cut into 4cm chunks

1 small swede, peeled and
  cut into 3cm chunks

2 carrots, peeled and cut
  into thick discs

1 onion, roughly chopped

1 yellow pepper, roughly
  chopped

20 juniper berries

5 garlic cloves

couple of sprigs of
  fresh thyme

½ lemon

1 cinnamon stick

200ml white wine

600ml chicken stock

hunk of bread, to serve

TURMERIC PASTE:

2 tsp ground turmeric

1 tsp smoked paprika

1 tsp cumin seeds

½ tsp smoked chilli powder

salt and freshly ground
  black pepper

Whole chicken in a slow cooker – moist, juicy and ready in several hours, Yes, please! This dish is so lovely and tasty and uses minimal equipment, time and energy. Again, the slow cooker saves the day – just put everything in, set the timer and you get a perfect dinner. You don't even need to boil the vegetables separately. And any leftovers can be used for chicken soup for your next meal too (see page 138).

To make the turmeric paste, mix the turmeric, paprika, cumin seeds and smoked chilli in a bowl. Add a little salt and pepper and a splash of water to create a spreadable paste.

Put the potatoes, swede, carrots, onion, pepper, juniper berries, garlic and a sprig of thyme into the bottom of a slow cooker bowl. If you don't have a slow cooker, add to a large ovenproof dish with a lid.

Put the lemon inside the chicken cavity along with a sprig of thyme. Rub the turmeric paste all over the chicken – on, in and under. (You may want to wear gloves to do this as it could make your hands quite yellow!) Sit the chicken on top of the potatoes and vegetables and pour the wine and the chicken stock around the edge. Drop in the cinnamon stick and add a pinch of salt and pepper. Give everything a jiggle, put on the lid and cook on low for 6½–7 hours until the potatoes are soft, and the chicken is pretty much falling off the bone.

If you don't have a slow cooker, put a lid on the ovenproof dish and cook in the oven at 130°C fan (150°C/300°F/Gas Mark 2) for 6½–7 hours. Check halfway through cooking in case you need to add a little more liquid.

Taste for seasoning and lift the chicken on to a chopping board. Roughly carve and pull the chicken apart.

Serve the potatoes and vegetables, topped with the melt-in-the-mouth chicken and pour over some of the beautiful cooking liquor. Use a hunk of bread to mop up the juices.

Leftover turmeric chicken, pearl barley + mushroom soup

SERVES 4

1 leftover roast chicken
  carcass (page 136)
250g chestnut mushrooms,
  finely chopped
25g dried porcini mushrooms
  soaked in boiling water
  then roughly chopped
1 onion, chopped
2 garlic cloves, crushed
2 carrots, peeled and cut
  into cubes
2 celery sticks, sliced
small bunch of fresh thyme
100g pearl barley
½ tsp garlic salt
½ tsp chilli flakes
½ tsp paprika
½ tsp mushroom powder
  (optional)
1 litre chicken stock
  (made with 2 stock cubes
  or bought fresh)
salt and freshly ground
  black pepper
100ml double cream

Another two for one recipe using the carcass and any leftover chicken from the recipe on page 136, which goes in with plenty of stock, vegetables and some pearl barley. A really warming winter soup, but if you use spring greens and veg it can be light enough for a spring broth. It's all about using seasonal veg with this one and you can also swap in brown rice or bulgur wheat for the pearl barley for a nourishing soup at any time of the year.

Place the chicken carcass in a saucepan and add water until it is about three quarters of the way up the chicken carcass. Set over a medium heat and bubble away until any leftover meat falls off the bones and it has broken down. Remove from the heat and leave to cool.

Strain the chicken stock through a sieve or strainer into another large saucepan. Set the stock aside and pick all of the cooked chicken meat off the bones and add to the stock. Discard all the bones and any non-edible bits. (Do not dump the lot down the sink as I once did!)

Add both types of mushrooms, onion, garlic, carrots, celery and thyme to the chicken stock and chicken.

Give the pearl barley a good rinse under cold water, then add to the stock mixture and stir. Stir through the garlic salt, chilli flakes, paprika, mushroom powder if using and a pinch of salt and pepper.

Top up with the chicken stock, stir, cover with a lid and set over a low-medium heat until the vegetables are soft, and the pearl barley is cooked with a little bite. This will take 40 minutes to 1 hour, so keep checking. Taste for seasoning and add salt and pepper if needed, then stir through the cream. Depending on how thick you like your soup, you may want to add a little more stock if you have it, but water works too.

Serve piping hot, next to an open fire if you can.

Smoky bean chilli

SERVES 8 (leftovers freeze well for another dinner)

coconut oil
1 red onion, chopped
4 garlic cloves, chopped
1 red pepper, deseeded and chopped
1 yellow pepper, deseeded and chopped
1 sweet potato, peeled and cubed
1 x 400g tin kidney beans, drained
1x 400g tin chickpeas, drained
1 x 400g tin black beans, drained
1 x 400g tin butter beans, drained
2 red chillies, finely chopped
1 tbsp tomato purée
2 tsp smoked paprika
2 tsp smoked chilli powder
1 tsp ground cumin
½ tsp ground cinnamon
1 tsp dried mixed herbs
4 fresh plum tomatoes, roughly chopped
1 x 400g tin chopped tomatoes
500ml vegetable stock
splash of Worcestershire sauce
splash of Tabasco sauce (optional)
couple of squares dark chocolate (minimum 70% cocoa solids for really good flavour)
salt and freshly ground black pepper

A perfect vegetarian chilli with all the beans! There is so much going on in this dish you won't even notice that it's meat free. The beauty of beans is that you can use whatever variety you like in this recipe. Lentils would be great too. Just remember if you are using dried beans, they may need soaking and cooking for longer.

If your slow cooker pot is ceramic and can be used on the hob, then remove from the holder, place over a medium heat and melt a large knob of the coconut oil. If not, or you don't have a slow cooker, use a large saucepan instead. Add the onion, garlic, peppers and sweet potato and fry for 5–6 minutes until everything starts to soften and turns a little golden.

Add the beans, fresh chillies and stir, then add the tomato purée and stir again. Sprinkle in the paprika, chilli powder, cumin, cinnamon and herbs and stir well. Add the fresh and tinned tomatoes and stir well. Allow to bubble away for a couple of minutes, then pour in the vegetable stock. Transfer the bowl to the slow cooker and cook on high for 4 hours or on low for 7 hours.

If you don't have a slow cooker, cook in the saucepan over a low heat for about 2 hours until the sauce has thickened, and all the beans are soft and lovely.

Give everything a really good stir, add the Worcestershire sauce and season with salt and pepper. Taste for spiciness and if you like it hot splash in some Tabasco. Drop in the dark chocolate and stir well.

Serve with couscous, a dollop of soured cream, a squeeze of lime and some fresh coriander. You can divide this into batches and freeze for up to one month for an easy-peasy dinner another night. Just defrost before heating on the hob.

Slow-cooked beef brisket in ale

SERVES 4

olive oil
800g–1kg beef brisket
1 courgette, sliced
125g whole baby button
   mushrooms, roughly
   chopped if larger
2 carrots, peeled and sliced
500g new potatoes, halved
   if large
1 red chilli, chopped
2 red onions, chopped
4 garlic cloves, roughly
   chopped
2 celery sticks, sliced
3 tbsp plain flour
few sprigs of fresh thyme
small bunch of fresh sage
330ml ale (I used BrewDog
   Punk IPA)
125ml beef stock (I used
   1 beef stock cube with
   125ml boiling water)
1 tsp smoked paprika
1 tbsp wholegrain mustard
splash of Worcestershire sauce
salt and freshly ground
   black pepper
hunk of bread, to serve

If you want warm, hearty and all the flavour, then here you go – this one's on me. Beef brisket is one of my favourite cuts of beef, especially cooked low and slow. It's tender, falls apart and takes on all the flavours from the ale, stock and herbs. This is a one-pot wonder – you can skip the pre-frying if you want, the browning just gives a little more flavour. Try swapping the beef for any other long cooking meat as well as switching up the vegetables according to the seasons.

This fits a large slow cooker, if you have a smaller one then slightly reduce the size of the brisket piece and the number of vegetables.

If your slow cooker pot is ceramic and can be used on the hob, then remove from the holder and add a good glug of oil over a high heat. If not or you're not using a slow cooker, then do the same with a large ovenproof dish with a lid.

Season the brisket all over with salt and pepper, then sear it in the very hot pan. You should get lovely brown sides very quickly. Remove the brisket from the pan and place on a plate.

Reduce the heat to medium, add a little more oil, then add the courgette, mushrooms, carrots, potatoes, chilli, red onions, garlic and celery. Using a wooden spoon, keep moving everything around until you get a little colour on the veg. Sprinkle over the flour and stir until all the ingredients are coated. Add the thyme and sage, then nestle the seared beef brisket on top. Pour over the ale and the stock and give the pan a good jiggle to mix. Most of the veg and brisket should just about be covered in the liquid.

You can also cook on high for 4—5 hours, if you're in a hurry!

Place the pan back into the slow cooker with the lid on and cook on low for 7–8 hours. The longer you cook the dish, the more melt in the mouth the brisket will be.

If you don't have a slow cooker, then cover the saucepan and cook in a low oven at 120°C fan (140°C/275°F/Gas Mark 1) for 7–8 hours. I found it did it good to give all the ingredients a little mix every now and again to make sure everything is getting cooked in the ale juice as everything seems to shrink down.

Add the paprika, mustard and Worcestershire sauce and mix through – the brisket will probably start breaking up at this point. Season with salt and pepper to taste.

Break up the brisket using two forks and serve in the sauce with the potatoes and veg and a hunk of bread to mop up the ale gravy.

Image overleaf →

Lamb, quinoa + feta

SERVES 4

olive oil

2 red onions, chopped

2 red, green, yellow or orange
  peppers, deseeded and
  chopped

1 carrot, peeled and chopped

3 garlic cloves, crushed

about 500–750g leftover roast
  lamb (page 161, this is based
  on approx. 1.5–2kg rolled
  and deboned lamb shoulder)

10 cherry tomatoes, halved

1 tbsp tomato purée

1 tsp smoked paprika

1 tsp cumin seeds

1 cinnamon stick

150g dried apricots, chopped

1 tsp chilli flakes or 2 red
  chillies, chopped

1 x 400g tin chopped tomatoes

500ml chicken stock
  (homemade or using stock
  cube and boiling water)

100g cooked quinoa

1 tbsp Worcestershire sauce

100g feta cheese

100g flaked almonds

250g packet of filo pastry
  (optional)

50g unsalted butter, melted
  (optional)

salt and freshly ground
  black pepper

Another recipe using leftovers from a previous day's cooking.
The only extra thing you need to do is plan a little extra meat,
but you'll be surprised how far the meat goes once mixed with the
other ingredients. This almost has a Middle Eastern vibe to it with
the spices, apricots and feta, and the filo pastry keeps it light and
fresh. You can also serve it without the pastry, straight from the
pot with a heap of salad.

Place a slow cooker pan or large saucepan over a medium heat and
add a glug of olive oil. Add the red onions, peppers and carrot
and fry for about 2 minutes until they start to soften, then add the
garlic and fry for a further 2 minutes.

Chop the leftover lamb into bite-sized chunks and add to the pan.
Fry for about 1 minute, then add the cherry tomatoes, tomato purée,
paprika, cumin seeds, cinnamon stick, apricots and chilli and give a
really good stir for about 1 minute over a low heat. Remove from the
heat and place into the slow cooker holder if using a slow cooker.

Add the tinned tomatoes, stock and season with a little salt and
pepper. Mix well and put on the lid. Cook on low for 6–7 hours or
high for 4–5 hours. If cooking on the hob, put a lid on the pan or
cover with foil and cook over a very low heat for 2–3 hours until the
lamb is falling apart.

Stir through the cooked quinoa and season to taste with salt,
pepper and Worcestershire sauce. At this point you can serve the
lamb sprinkled with feta and almonds alongside a salad, spinach
leaves or cooked courgettes or if you want to make the pie, preheat
the oven to 160°C fan (180°C/350°F/Gas Mark 4).

Continued overleaf →

Place the cooked lamb mix into an ovenproof dish and crumble over the feta and half the flaked almonds.

Take the filo pastry and gently scrunch up the individual sheets, then place the pastry scrunches on top of the filling. Continue until the mix is completely covered in filo – you can bunch it together. Brush the melted butter all over the jagged filo scrunches and sprinkle over the remaining almonds – they should fall into the gaps.

Bake for about 15 minutes until the filo is golden and crispy. The filling was already hot, so it is just the filo that needs cooking. (If the filling is cold, gently heat up before topping with filo.) Serve hot with whatever you like or just on its own!

If you don't have any leftover roast lamb, you can buy boneless lamb shoulder and use that instead.

Slow-cooked pork, celeriac + apple

SERVES 4

olive oil
knob of butter
1 large onion, chopped
2 leeks, chopped
1 celeriac, peeled and cut
    into 1.5cm chunks
4 garlic cloves, chopped
1 tsp fennel seeds
small bunch of fresh sage
few sprigs of fresh thyme
about 800g leftover roast
    pork shoulder (page 163),
    cut into bite-sized chunks
450ml dry apple cider
1 tbsp wholegrain mustard
500ml chicken stock
2 Bramley cooking apples
salt and freshly ground
    black pepper

Buy a slightly bigger joint of pork for your Sunday (or any day) roast dinner and you should have leftovers for this succulent, almost pulled, pork dish. Cut the pork into chunks and as it cooks, the meat becomes melt in the mouth. The addition of the apples later on means they still have a little crunch as well as tang. This recipe really is all about making cooking comforting food as easy as possible.

If you have a slow cooker, place the slow cooker pan over a medium heat. If not, place a saucepan over a medium heat and add a glug of olive oil and the butter. Add the chopped vegetables and garlic and fry for 4–5 minutes until they start to soften and gain a little colour. Add the fennel seeds, sage and thyme and mix well.

Add the pork and cook for 2–3 minutes, stirring until everything starts to colour.

Pour in the cider and bubble away for 2–3 minutes. Stir in the mustard and top up with the chicken stock. Season with salt and pepper, place the pan in the slow cooker and cook on low for 6–7 hours in total.

Peel and core the apples and cut into chunks. After 3–4 hours of cooking, stir the apples into the pork mixture and cook for a further 3 hours. (You can add them at the start, but they will just be a little softer.)

If you don't have a slow cooker, then you can cook the whole dish in a large saucepan with the lid on. Simmer for 2–3 hours over a low heat until the vegetables are soft, and the pork is almost pulled-pork-like. Then add the prepared apples and simmer for a further 30 minutes until soft.

Taste and add more seasoning if needed. Remove the sage and thyme stalks and serve with a mountain of mash or use as a pie filling.

Mushroom, spinach + sweetcorn risotto

SERVES 4

50g unsalted butter

300g mixed mushrooms, such
as chestnut, closed cup,
oyster, portobello, cep or
straw, chopped into different
sized pieces

25g dried porcini mushrooms,
soaked and softened in
boiling water, drained

3 shallots, thinly sliced

3 garlic cloves, crushed

1 tsp dried thyme

1 tsp dried sage

250g risotto rice

100g pearl barley

1 tsp mushroom powder
(optional – you can finely blitz
dried porcinis for this too)

250ml white wine

750ml vegetable stock (made
from 2 vegetable stock cubes
and 750ml boiling water)

100g sweetcorn (I used
frozen and defrosted)

100g baby spinach

100g Swiss chard, chopped
(optional)

50g Parmesan cheese,
finely grated, plus extra
to serve (optional)

salt and freshly ground
black pepper

Risotto, so loved, but such an effort having to stand and stir and watch and stir the whole time! Not this one. Put it all in, walk away and then serve. If you want to give it a little stir throughout and check the flavour, then I don't blame you, but this risotto is as easy as it gets. There are loads of flavour possibilities too – sun-dried tomatoes and fresh basil or try dropping in some prawns near the end for a seafood twist. Don't forget the Parmesan to serve.

If you have a slow cooker, place the bowl of the slow cooker over a low-medium heat and add the butter, then the mixed mushrooms, softened porcini and shallots. Stir constantly for 3–4 minutes until the mushrooms and shallots start to soften, but not colour too much. Add the garlic, dried thyme and sage and fry for 3 minutes.

Add the risotto rice and pearl barley and stir so all of the grains are coated in the buttery mushroom liquid. Add the mushroom powder, if using, and fry for a couple of minutes. Pour in the white wine and bubble for a minute, then top up with the vegetable stock. Mix and season with salt and pepper. Put on the lid, place the bowl in the slow cooker and cook on high for 1 hour 15 minutes. Check after 1 hour to see if it needs a little more liquid and to see if the rice and pearl barley are cooked.

If you do not have a slow cooker, then use a large frying pan for the above steps but add the stock a little at a time, stirring constantly, then leave the pan on the heat and mix continually until all of the liquid has been absorbed and the rice is cooked. This should take 20–30 minutes.

Once the risotto is cooked, remove from the heat and stir through the sweetcorn, spinach and chard, if using. Leave for a further 15 minutes. The heat will wilt the spinach and cook the chard. Stir though the Parmesan. Once served, the risotto should sit on the plate then slowly settle – not so runny it's like soup and not so thick it stands up! Season to taste. Serve with additional Parmesan for any cheese fans.

Leek + potato soup with Stilton croutons

MAKES 2 BIG PORTIONS OR 4 SMALLER ONES

2 large leeks
1 large onion
4 garlic cloves
1 celery stick
large knob of butter
olive oil
4–5 potatoes, peeled and
   chopped
small bunch of fresh sage,
   plus a few leaves to serve
½ tsp dried thyme
splash of white wine (optional)
850ml vegetable stock
the heels of a loaf of brown,
   white or granary bread
   (uncut)
100g Stilton cheese
salt and freshly ground
   black pepper

One of my favourite soups – hearty, flavoursome and the Stilton croutons take it to the next level. So lazy you don't even need to dip the bread in, it's already in there for you. This can be frozen in batches and taken out as you need it on those grey days when you don't feel like cooking.

Trim the ends of the leeks and wash them before slicing into 1cm rings. Roughly chop the onion, garlic and celery.

If your slow cooker pot is ceramic and can be used on the hob, then remove from the holder and add the butter and a glug of olive oil. If not, or you don't have a slow cooker, then add the butter and oil to a saucepan. Add the leeks, onion, celery and garlic and sweat over a low heat until they start to get soft and shiny but not take on too much colour.

Add the potatoes, sage and thyme, mix well and cook for 2–3 minutes. Add a splash of wine if using and allow to bubble away for a further 2–3 minutes, then top up with the stock and season with salt and pepper.

Place into the slow cooker and cook on high for 3–4 hours or low for 6–7 hours until the potatoes break down if squished with a spoon. You can also cook the soup in a pan on the hob over a medium heat for 45 minutes to 1 hour until the potatoes and veg are soft.

To make the croutons, preheat the oven to 170°C fan (190°C/375°F/ Gas Mark 5) and tear the bread into large bite-sized chunks. Spread a little Stilton on top of each chunk, place on a baking tray and drizzle with olive oil. Bake for 10–12 minutes until the bread is golden and crunchy and the Stilton is melted and bubbling.

Continued overleaf →

Turn the slow cooker off and remove the bowl (if cooking on the hob, remove the pan from the heat). Using a stick blender, if you have one, blitz the soup until it forms a coarse purée. If you prefer it completely smooth, then blitz it for a little longer but I quite like a few lumpy bits. You can also use a food processor or blender but do not put the lid on as the heat will cause it to explode and I'm pretty sure you do not want hot soup everywhere! Taste and add salt and pepper if it needs them.

Pour the soup into bowls, top with a couple of the jagged Stilton croutons, a little drizzle of olive oil and a sprinkle of torn sage leaves.

This soup can be stored in the fridge for two days or portioned up and frozen for up to a month.

Defrost before reheating.

Coconut, spinach + pistachio chana dhal

SERVES 4 AS A MAIN OR 8 AS A SIDE

1 tbsp coconut oil
1 large onion, diced
5 garlic cloves, finely sliced
1 red chilli, chopped
1 green chilli, chopped
thumb-sized piece fresh ginger, peeled and finely diced
2 tsp cumin seeds
1 tsp mustard seeds
350g dried split chickpeas (chana dhal)
2 tsp ground turmeric
1 tsp hot madras curry powder
400ml hot vegetable stock
1 x 400ml tin coconut milk
2 bay leaves
1 tsp chilli flakes (optional)
200g baby spinach (frozen works too, just defrost first and remove excess water)
50g pistachios, chopped
50g pumpkin seeds
small bunch of coriander, chopped (optional)
salt and freshly ground black pepper
cooked rice, naan or chapattis, to serve

I have eaten so many dhals and I often try to make my own at home. Another favourite dish of mine is a saag, so I wanted to combine the two and then added some pistachios for texture. The fragrances that come from this dish cooking really do leave your mouth watering. A warming, sharing meal that everyone can dive into, mopping up with breads.

If your slow cooker pot is ceramic and can be used on the hob, then remove from the holder, place over a medium heat and add the coconut oil, then the onion, garlic, chillies and ginger. If you don't have a slow cooker, then add the ingredients to a saucepan. Add the cumin and mustard seeds and stir for 5–6 minutes until the onion starts to soften and brown slightly and the seeds begin to smell beautifully aromatic.

Rinse the dried split chickpeas really well in cold water, then add to the onion mixture. Remove from the heat and stir through, coating the split chickpeas in the onion mixture. Stir through the turmeric and curry powder and season with salt and pepper.

Pour in the hot vegetable stock along with the coconut milk and stir well. Drop in the bay leaves and place the lid on. Transfer to a slow cooker and cook for 4 hours on high or 7–8 hours on low. If you do not have a slow cooker, cover the saucepan and cook over a low heat for 1½–2 hours, stirring occasionally.

Stir and taste. Add a little more seasoning if needed and the chilli flakes if you like a little heat. Stir in the spinach and cook for a further 15 minutes.

Put the pistachios and pumpkin seeds in a dry frying pan and fry over a low-medium heat until lightly toasted.

Serve the dhal with a sprinkling of the toasted seeds, nuts and coriander, if using, along with rice, naan or chapattis.

Overnight porridge with apple, seeds + goji berries

SERVES 2

½ cup jumbo oats

1½ cups oat milk

2 tbsp mixed seeds (I used pumpkin, poppy, sunflower and flax seeds)

2 tbsp dried goji berries

pinch of salt

2 cardamom pods, squeezed so the pods are slightly open

1 eating apple

You've heard of overnight oats, but they are always cold, and I want hot porridge, but as I'm so disorganised and late for everything (I blame the ADHD), I rarely have time to make it in the morning or I do it in the microwave and then it overspills, and I make a mess (again I blame ADHD). This recipe solves all of that. Pop the porridge on before bed, wake up, grate in your apple and add whatever else you want, and boom, breakfast is served. The goji berries make it a little bit pink, but pretty too.

Put the oats in a heatproof bowl and pour in the oat milk and ½ cup of water. Stir well. Add the seeds, goji berries and salt and mix together. Drop in the cardamom pods.

Transfer the mixture to the bowl of a slow cooker and carefully pour in water until it reaches about three quarters of the way up the bowl. Cover with the lid and cook on low for 7 hours. (If you happen to wake up in the night, then give it a little stir, if not don't worry.)

If you don't have a slow cooker, you can leave the porridge mix covered in the fridge overnight for cold overnight oats. To serve, add the grated apple and a dollop of yoghurt.

Stir the overnight porridge really well in the morning. You may need to add a splash of water or more oat milk if it's too thick.

Remove the cardamom pods. Grate in the apple and stir well. The apple may add extra liquid to the porridge so just be aware of this. Serve hot.

Stewed fruit

SERVES 6

5 large Bramley apples,
    peeled, cored and chopped
    into large chunks
1kg rhubarb, topped and tailed
    and cut into 5cm pieces
100g dried cranberries
200g golden caster sugar
zest and juice of 1 orange
1 cinnamon stick
2 sprigs of fresh rosemary

Stewed fruit in the slow cooker saves having to stand next to the hob as you can just leave it to take care of itself. It's perfect for crumbles, pies, yoghurt topping, or just on its own as an after-dinner treat.

Place the apples and rhubarb into a slow cooker and sprinkle over the cranberries, sugar and orange zest and pour in the orange juice. Mix well and add a splash of water if the mix looks a little dry. Drop in the cinnamon stick and rosemary sprigs. Cook on low for 4 hours. Check after 3 hours of cooking, give it a little stir and add a drop more water if needed.

If you don't have a slow cooker you can do this in a saucepan over a low heat and simmer for 45 minutes to 1 hour.

This is perfect as a crumble base or pie filling, or served with cream, custard or yoghurt. It will keep in the fridge for two days but can be frozen for up to one month.

How about adding this to your Overnight porridge?

Chocolate, caramel + chia seed rice pudding

SERVES 4

50g unsalted butter, plus
  25g for greasing
150g pudding rice
700ml whole milk
500ml double cream
50g light soft brown sugar
½ tsp ground cinnamon
50g chia seeds
100g dark chocolate chips
  or dark chocolate (minimum
  70% cocoa solids), chopped
100g caramel
½ tsp sea salt flakes

Possibly the naughtiest, sweetest rice pudding you'll taste and probably the easiest. Such an old-fashioned dessert, but there's so much you can add to make it interesting. You could even keep it plain and give everyone their own options to top it with. Or simply swirl through the chocolate and caramel and get ready for the sweet-toothed to fall in love.

Grease the inside of the slow cooker basin with 25g of the butter, then add the pudding rice. Pour in the milk and cream and mix. Stir through the sugar, cinnamon and chia seeds, then add the rest of the butter. Place the lid on the slow cooker and cook for 3–3½ hours on high or 6–6½ hours on low. You will need to give it a stir to break up the rice a little bit and prevent sticking occasionally.

If you don't have a slow cooker, follow the above instructions in an ovenproof dish, cover and cook in the oven at 140°C fan (160°C/325°F/Gas Mark 3) for 3–3½ hours or 120°C fan (140°C/275°F/Gas Mark 1) for 5–5½ hours.

Make sure the rice is cooked through and the whole thing is not too claggy and thick. Stir well and divide between bowls, sprinkle over some chocolate chips, drizzle over some caramel and sprinkle with a little sea salt.

Enjoy hot, warm or cold with that lovely bit of skin on top.

You can add a little more milk at this point, if needed.

Nostalgia food

SAVOURY:

Roast lamb – 161

Roast topside of beef – 162

Roast pork shoulder with crackling – 163

Brown butter macaroni cheese – 164

Sausage patty breakfast bagels – 167

Proper pub beer-battered fish and chips with tartare sauce – 168

Sweet potato and ham hock hash – 172

SWEET:

Jam tarts – 174

Chocolate mint toothpaste – 175

Tottenham cake – 176

Angel cake – 179

Cherry and almond spotted dick – 181

School dinner coconut and jam sponge – 182

Chocolate and apricot sponge with chocolate custard – 184

Tiramisu bread and butter pudding with Baileys cream – 187

Speculoos and jelly Arctic roll – 189

Chocolate orange roly-poly with cinnamon custard – 192

Treacle, pecan and pear tart – 195

Toffee apples and pears – 196

ONE OF THE THINGS I talk about a lot is food that sparks nostalgia and brings back happy memories. This might be your favourite dinner your mum used to make, the Sunday roast and perfect puddings your Nan cooked when you went to stay, that birthday treat you still remember from when you were five, or a school-dinner pudding that you may or may not have eaten two portions of because you told the dinner lady your mam said it was OK! And the fact that my Nan Ivy survived on a diet of chocolates and biscuits and she was fine!

The smell, the taste, the process of making it, how those memories flood back as you remove your bake from the oven, getting enveloped in the hot cake's steam and not being able to wait until you tuck in – this is all precious and the stuff of life! The way food can make you feel, sparking emotions from happy times, thoughts and feelings – this can be therapy in itself. We saw this happen with my grandad who had Alzheimer's – food would always bring him back to us.

What are your favourite food memories? How does food make you feel? What are your earliest food recollections? Mine is being at my Nan's and dragging the dining chair through to stand next to her while she baked and her giving me the pastry cut-offs to make jam tarts. See, I'm smiling – food memories should do that, always. Don't have any food memories? Start making your own, start sharing and keep smiling.

Roast lamb

SERVES 4-6 PEOPLE
with leftovers for Lamb,
quinoa and feta (page 145)

2-2.5kg boneless rolled
    leg of lamb
olive oil
5-6 sprigs of fresh rosemary
4 garlic cloves
1 lemon, halved
salt and freshly ground
    black pepper

I think cooking lamb worries some people and I hope this gives you confidence when roasting lamb joints. Lamb goes beautifully with mint, but it can be so much more, and I want you to use it for the wonderful flavour it has, especially in the spring. British lamb is one of the best pieces of meat we have, so use it and enjoy it with family or friends. Even if you just want to treat yourself – do it. It's what self-care is all about.

Preheat the oven to 200°C fan (220°C/425°F/Gas Mark 7).

Place the lamb in a fairly high-sided baking tray to catch all the juice and fat.

Rub a little oil all over the lamb and give it a good rub of salt and pepper.

Scatter over some rosemary and poke the garlic cloves into small slits in the meat and wedge the lemon underneath.

The general rule to for roast lamb is to cook it for 20 minutes per 500g for rare or 25 minutes per 500g for more well done. Roast for 20 minutes, then reduce the oven temperature to 180°C fan (200°C/400°F/Gas Mark 6). Measure the internal temperature by probing the middle of the meat with a meat thermometer and leaving for 1 minute. The internal temperature should read 50–55°C.

Remove from the oven, cover very loosely with foil and rest for at least 45 minutes before serving.

Roasting Meat

Always remove the meat from the fridge about 30 minutes to 1 hour before cooking so it comes up to room temperature.

Roast topside of beef

SERVES 4

1.5–2kg topside of beef
butter
1 bulb of garlic, halved
2 carrots, halved lengthways
small bunch of fresh thyme
salt and freshly ground
   black pepper

Topside is the pub's preferred cut of choice and we serve it beautifully rare, so it melts in the mouth. Leftovers are perfect for a huge doorstop hot roast beef, horseradish and flattened Yorkshire pudding sandwich with gravy to dunk it in. Or perfect in a stew with fat dumplings. Please excuse me, I seem to be drooling!

Preheat the oven to 200°C fan (220°C/425°F/Gas Mark 7).

Place the beef in a fairly high-sided baking tray to catch all the juice.

Rub some butter all over the beef and give it a good rub of salt and pepper.

Lift the beef up and sit on top of the garlic, carrots and thyme.

Cook for 20 minutes per 500g for rare and 25 minutes per 500g for medium. Cook for 20 minutes, then reduce the oven temperature to 180°C fan (200°C/400°F/Gas Mark 6). Measure the internal temperature by probing the middle of the meat with a meat thermometer and leaving for 1 minute before reading. The internal temperature should read 45–55°C. It's worth remembering the end of the beef will be more well done than the middle section. Something for everyone!

Remove from the oven, cover very loosely with foil and leave to rest for 45 minutes before serving.

Roast pork shoulder with crackling

SERVES 4–6 PEOPLE
with leftovers for Slow-cooked pork, celeriac and apple (page 147)

2–2.5kg pork shoulder, boned
small bunch of fresh sage
1 onion, halved
salt and freshly ground
    black pepper

Don't scrimp on the salt on the crackling!

There are so many ways to cook a joint of pork depending on the cut, if it has the bone in, the size, if you want it spiced or with crackling. I'm not trying to reinvent the wheel here or teach you things you don't already know, this is just my easy way of getting beautifully tender pork and having enough for pie filling the next day. A deboned shoulder joint is my preferred cut. Always double check your weights and use a meat thermometer to check internal temperatures if you are not sure.

Preheat the oven to 160°C fan (180°C/350°F/Gas Mark 4).

With a very sharp knife, score the pork skin with a criss-cross pattern, then rub in a good amount of salt and pepper.

Place the sage and onion in a high-sided baking tray and top with the pork.

Roast for 25 minutes per 500g, plus an extra 30 minutes. Measure the internal temperature by probing the middle of the meat with a meat thermometer. The internal temperature should be 65–70°C. The juices of the pork should run almost clear or very slightly pink when the meat is poked when cooked.

Brown butter macaroni cheese

SERVES 4

250g dried macaroni
50g unsalted butter
100g plain flour
700ml whole milk
150g Emmental cheese,
    grated
150g gherkins or cornichons,
    roughly chopped
4 spring onions, roughly
    chopped
100g jalapeño chillies,
    roughly chopped
150g Brie
salt and freshly ground
    black pepper

TOPPING:
25g unsalted butter
40g panko breadcrumbs
    (or blitz up day-old bread)
small bunch of fresh
    flat-leaf parsley
small bunch of fresh dill
1 garlic cloves

Do I need to say more?! This is the best macaroni cheese I've ever tasted and, believe me, I've tasted a lot. It's the ultimate comfort food. Mam used to make it in bulk and freeze it so I could take it to university and my housemates were always jealous. This version is next level though – tart with gherkins, a little kick of heat and nutty from the brown butter and all the cheese. If you've got some crisps lying around, scrunch them up and whack them on top too! You're welcome.

Preheat the oven to 160°C fan (180°C/350°F/Gas Mark 4).

To make the topping, melt the butter in a small saucepan over a medium heat. Once it has melted, leave it to foam and then turn a rich dark brown colour, scraping the bottom of the pan so it doesn't burn. Remove from the heat.

Blitz the breadcrumbs, parsley, dill and garlic together in a food processor. Mix this through the brown butter and set aside.

Bring a large saucepan of salted water to the boil over a high heat and add the macaroni. Cook until al dente (with a slight bite as it will finish cooking in the oven). Drain and set aside.

Add the butter to a large sauce pan and melt over a medium heat. Once melted, allow the butter to foam and turn a golden to rich brown colour – use a spatula or wooden spoon to scrape any bits off the bottom of the pan to prevent it burning. Add the flour and mix to cook out the flour – this may take a couple of minutes. Gradually add the milk, stirring constantly, until it is all incorporated and then continue to mix until the sauce (the roux) has completely thickened and coats the back of a wooden spoon.

While the sauce is still hot, stir through the Emmental until melted. Stir the gherkins, spring onions and jalapeños through the cheese sauce and add salt and pepper to taste. Tip the cooked macaroni into the cheese sauce and fold through until evenly combined. Tip into a 25 x 30cm ovenproof dish.

Slice the Brie lengthways and lay across the top of the macaroni cheese, then sprinkle over the brown butter breadcrumbs. Bake for 25–30 minutes until the edges are bubbling and the breadcrumbs are golden brown. Serve hot and gooey.

Sausage patty breakfast bagels

SERVES 4

8 good-quality pork
    sausages (check the
    ingredients for seasoning)
½ tsp dried sage
splash of Worcestershire sauce
couple drops of Tabasco sauce
4 eggs
knob of butter, plus extra
    for frying
50g mozzarella cheese,
    grated
4 bagels of your choice
    (I like seeded)
4 slices of American cheese
salt and freshly ground
    black pepper

During lockdown it was my Mam's birthday and I decided to make her breakfast. We took it round with Buck's Fizz and sat along the drive while we ate these McSusie's together. It was a little bit of light relief and made my Mam smile on her special day. It's not the poshest of breakfasts, but it was quick and easy and made us think of happy times.

Squeeze the sausage meat out of the skins into a large bowl. Add a little salt and pepper, the dried sage, a splash of Worcestershire sauce and a drop or two of Tabasco and mix together. Get in there with your hands and squeeze everything together. Form the sausage meat into four burger-shaped patties and place on a plate in the fridge for 10 minutes.

Mix the eggs in a bowl with a little salt and pepper, the butter and the grated mozzarella. Slice the bagels in half.

Heat a large frying pan over a medium heat and add the sausage patties. Fry for 2–3 minutes on each side until you get a nice browned char on the outside and the meat is cooked. Place, covered, in a low oven to keep warm while you prepare the rest of the ingredients.

Wipe out the pan, add a little knob of butter and set over a medium-high heat. When the butter has melted, swirl the pan around and pour in the egg and mozzarella mixture. Using a spatula, give the eggs a little mix, drawing the outside in and allow to cook as one big eggy pancake. When the top has just about set, flip over to cook the other side for 2–3 minutes. Divide into four even pieces.

Toast the bagel halves.

Layer the bagels with a slice of American cheese on the bottom followed by a sausage patty and then top with an egg pancake. Add a squirt of sauce if you like (I don't have any, so I have extra cheese!) then the bagel top. Enjoy!

Proper pub beer-battered fish + chips with tartare sauce

SERVES 2

4–6 potatoes, preferably
  Maris piper
2 pieces of tail fillet of
  sustainable white fish, such
  as haddock (small fish works
  well too, such as sardines or
  mackerel)
90g plain flour, plus 3 tbsp
⅔ tsp bicarbonate soda
½ tsp seaweed flakes (optional)
160ml lager
sunflower oil
salt flakes
small bunch of fresh chives,
  finely snipped
1 lemon, cut into wedges

TARTARE SAUCE:

5 tbsp mayonnaise
50g gherkins or cornichons,
  finely chopped
1 tbsp capers, finely chopped
1 small shallot, finely chopped
zest and juice of 1 lemon
small bunch of fresh flat-leaf
  parsley, finely chopped
salt and freshly ground
  black pepper

A great British staple and a fixture on the menu at our pub, The Green Man. In fact, it's one of our bestselling dishes. Thick, fresh pieces of haddock, lightly dusted, then dipped in bubbly beer batter and fried until golden and crisp alongside triple-cooked chips that are more like rectangular slabs of potato that make people come back time and time again. Change up your fish – try cod in season, sustainable pollock or even smoked haddock (this was a happy accident) but absolutely no peas for me please.

Peel or thinly slice off alternate strips of each potato so there is a little skin left. (If the potatoes are muddy, then give them a good scrub before peeling.) Slice the potatoes into thick, chunky chips.

Put the potatoes in a saucepan of salted water. Place over a high heat and bring to the boil. Once boiling, reduce the heat slightly and cook until you can just poke through the potatoes easily with a knife. Drain the potatoes and carefully tip out on to a tray lined with a clean tea towel. Wrap the edges up over the potatoes. Leave to cool.

Put the flour, bicarbonate of soda in a bowl and add the seaweed, if using. Pour in the lager and whisk until there are no lumps and you have a smooth, thick batter. Set aside to rest while you make the tartare sauce and chips.

Add all the tartare sauce ingredients to a bowl and mix together until combined. Season to taste with salt and pepper. Set aside.

If you do not have a deep-fat fryer, pour the sunflower oil into a heavy-based saucepan until you have about 10–12cm in the bottom. Set over a medium heat and heat to 180°C (350°F). If you don't have a thermometer, you can also test the oil is ready by dropping in a square of bread – if it floats and turns golden quickly, then the oil is ready. If using a deep-fat fryer, set to 180°C (350°F) and wait until at temperature.

You may need to fry the chips in batches.

Carefully using a frying basket or slotted spoon, place the potatoes into the hot oil and fry until they float and are a lovely golden brown. Remove with a slotted spoon or fryer basket and tip on to a plate lined with kitchen paper to drain off excess oil. Transfer to a large bowl, sprinkle with salt flakes and the chives and toss together.

Put the 3 tablespoons of flour in a bowl. Holding on to the thin tail end of a fish fillet, coat it in the flour, then dip into the batter, ensuring the whole piece of fish is covered. Very carefully lower the fish into the hot oil. Repeat with second fillet. Fry for 3–4 minutes on each side, carefully turning in the oil. (The cooking time varies depending on the thickness and size of the fish – thicker fish may need a little longer and sardines or mackerel will need significantly less.)

Remove the fish from the oil and set on some kitchen paper to drain any excess oil. Sprinkle with salt flakes.

Serve the fish proudly sat on top of a mountain of salty chips with a big dollop of tartare sauce. Add a wedge of lemon and you are set to go! You may notice no peas – that's because no one needs that sort of negativity on their plates!

Image overleaf →

Sweet potato + ham hock hash

SERVES 2

2 large sweet potatoes,
  scrubbed
olive oil
2 red or green chillies, sliced
½ red onion, sliced
½ courgette, sliced
160g cooked ham hock,
  shredded
100g baby spinach
2 eggs
salt and freshly ground
  black pepper

I remember both my Nan and Mam making corned beef hash with the stuff from a tin as a regular weeknight meal and my dad loving it, but he had to have a runny fried egg on top. Nowadays you get all sorts of hash on menus with everything from proper corned beef and chorizo to black pudding, so now you have my version with cubes of sweet potato, spinach, tender ham hock and, of course, the runny fried egg.

Preheat the oven to 160°C fan (180°C/350°F/Gas Mark 4).

Prick the sweet potatoes all over, place on a baking tray and bake for 30 minutes.

Remove from oven and leave to cool slightly, then chop into 2cm cubes.

Heat a large frying pan over a medium heat, add a glug of oil followed by the sweet potatoes. Bash the sweet potatoes up a little and fry for 2–3 minutes. Add the chillies, onion and courgette and fry for 4–5 minutes until softened and getting a little colour.

Add the ham hock and cook for 4–5 minutes, stirring constantly. Stir through the spinach until it has wilted down. Season to taste with salt and pepper.

In a separate saucepan, fry the eggs in a little oil over a medium heat until the white is set, but the yolk is runny. Alternatively, you can poach the eggs according to the instructions on page 73.

Divide hash between two plates and top with a runny egg each. Serve.

Jam tarts

MAKES 12

100g golden caster sugar
100g unsalted butter
3 egg yolks
200g plain flour, plus extra
    for dusting
pinch of salt
50g hazelnuts, chopped
icing sugar, for dusting

**BLACKBERRY AND
APPLE JAM:**
200g Bramley apples, peeled,
    cored and chopped
150g golden caster sugar
zest and juice of 1 lemon
200g blackberries

These were one of the first things I made with my Nan – she used to give me the pastry cut offs from a pie she was making to fill with sticky jam. These are a little fancier as you make your own pastry and jam. So, you get the simplicity, but also the satisfaction. If you want to make them with curd, then go for it or add a blob of peanut butter to the jam to make peanut butter and jelly tarts. Cheeky.

Preheat the oven to 180°C fan (200°C/400°F/Gas Mark 6).

To make the pastry, beat together the sugar and butter in a large bowl with an electric mixer until pale and fluffy. Beat in the egg yolks, followed by the flour and salt. Bring together with your hands to form a ball of dough. Flatten this slightly, then wrap in clingfilm and transfer to the fridge to chill for 20 minutes.

Roll out the pastry on a floured work surface until it is 3mm thick. Cut out rounds using a fluted or round cutter slightly bigger than the holes in your muffin tin. You should get about 12 discs – if you have any pastry left, cut out some mini stars or hearts to place on top of the tarts.

Gently press the pastry discs into the tin holes – you can use the rounded end of a rolling pin dipped in flour to do this. Chill in the fridge for 10 minutes.

To make the jam, put the apples, sugar and lemon zest and juice in a small saucepan over a low heat to dissolve the sugar and allow the apples to soften, stirring occasionally. This should take about 10 minutes. Remove from the heat, drop in the blackberries and stir.

Spoon some of the apple and blackberry jam into each pastry case, sprinkle over some hazelnuts and top with a little pastry star or heart, if you have one. Bake for 15–17 minutes until the jam is bubbling and the pastry is golden.

Remove the tarts from the oven and leave to cool slightly in the tin, then transfer to a wire rack to cool completely. Dust with icing sugar and serve cold as a treat or warm, drowned in custard.

Chocolate mint toothpaste

SERVES 4-6

1 x 250g packet of
   ready-made filo pastry
125g unsalted butter, 50g
   melted and 75g softened
150g golden caster sugar
25g mint hot chocolate
   powder (I used Options
   Mint Madness)
20g cocoa powder
225g milk powder
150ml warm water
small bunch of fresh mint
25g icing sugar

The famous or infamous Bedfordshire school tart-type pudding. My friends from school all absolutely love this weird grainy treat. I had to pimp it up a little as, to be honest, it's not my fave. But I often get asked if I make it, so girls this one is for you! It's usually known as Chocolate Toothpaste, so obviously I had to make it mint flavoured.

Preheat the oven to 160°C fan (180°C/350°F/Gas Mark 4).

Lay one sheet of filo pastry in a shallow muffin tin about 13cm diameter. Brush with melted butter and lay in another sheet at a different angle, making sure the edges stick up like a shallow dish, then brush on more butter and lay on a third sheet and repeat for a fourth. Repeat until you have used all the filo pastry and you have between 4–6 pastry cases. Bake for 12–15 minutes until golden and crisp. Remove from the oven and leave to cool.

Whisk the softened butter and the caster sugar together in a bowl until pale and fluffy. Add the mint hot chocolate powder and cocoa and mix together well.

In a separate bowl mix together the powdered milk and warm water until combined

Pour into the chocolate mixture and whisk together. Chop up a few mint leaves very finely and fold through the mix. Pour into the baked filo cases and place in the fridge overnight to set.

When ready to serve, top with a fresh sprig of mint and a dusting of icing sugar.

Don't hate me Bedford for tweaking an old classic!

Tottenham cake

MAKES 9 BIG HUNKS OF SPONGE OR 12 SMALLER

20g desiccated coconut or sprinkles (optional)
160g golden caster sugar
160g unsalted butter
3 eggs
170g self-raising flour
zest of 1 lemon
splash of whole milk
50g fresh or frozen berries of your choice (I used raspberries and blackberries)
130g icing sugar

If it's too thick then add a couple of drops of water at a time.

Being a North London Tottenham girl born and bred, this cake makes me very happy indeed, and although many a football fan will turn their nose up at the name, that soon changes when they taste it. I believe the name comes from the fact that the pink icing was originally coloured using mulberries found in the grounds of the Tottenham Friends' Meeting House and sold for a penny a slice! For my icing, I've used raspberries and blackberries to give a gorgeous pinky purple colour and flavour.

Preheat the oven to 160°C fan (180°C/350°F/Gas Mark 4) and line a 25cm square cake tin with greaseproof paper.

Place the desiccated coconut (if using) on a tray and toast in the oven for about 5 minutes until it is starting to turn golden brown.

Put the sugar and butter in a large bowl and mix together using a free-standing electric mixer or handheld electric mixer (or bowl and wooden spoon), for about 2 minutes until pale and fluffy. Add the eggs and mix on a high speed. Tip in the flour and lemon zest and mix to combine. Add the milk and mix to combine. The cake batter should slowly drop off the mixer.

Spoon the batter into the prepared tin and bake for 20–25 minutes until risen and golden brown or a skewer inserted into the centre comes out clean. Turn out on to a wire rack and leave to cool completely.

Smash up the berries and pass the mixture through a sieve and add the strained berry liquid to the icing sugar, then mix together until you have a thick, smooth icing.

Once the sponge is completely cool, pour over the berry icing and sprinkle on the toasted desiccated coconut or sprinkles (if using). Cut into squares and enjoy the memories of your childhood and the mighty Spurs (or any other team you support!).

This keeps for two days stored in an airtight container.

Angel cake

MAKES ABOUT 8 SLICES
but my brother can eat the
whole thing to himself

CAKE:
175g unsalted butter
175g golden caster sugar
3 eggs
175g self-raising flour
rose water
pink food colouring gel
zest and juice 1 lemon
yellow food colouring gel
1 tsp amaretto

JAM:
200g raspberries
100g golden caster sugar
zest and juice 1 lemon

BUTTERCREAM:
50g very soft unsalted butter
100g icing sugar, plus extra
   for dusting
splash of double cream

Eating this turns you into an angel. (Disclaimer – it doesn't really!) My brother Ben could eat almost an entire one of these (I also ate my fair share), and it was his favourite growing up. He may not appreciate the fact I've added jam to the layers, but the real struggle was deciding which colour went where. I'm still not sure I made the right choice, so if you think it needs changing, then go for it. You could also change the colours completely should you wish, and you can leave the jam out if you like too.

To make the jam, put the raspberries, sugar and lemon zest and juice in a saucepan and cook over a medium heat until the sugar has dissolved. Leave to bubble away for 15–20 minutes until thickened and starting to set when cooled You can check it's ready to set by placing a saucer in the freezer and then placing a blob of jam on the frozen saucer – if the jam wrinkles when you run your finger through it, then it's ready. Remove from the heat and leave to cool completely.

To make the sponges, preheat oven to 160°C fan (180°C/350°F/ Gas Mark 4) and use a large piece of greaseproof paper to create three equal sections in a rectangular baking tray. You can use some foil underneath to create a small barrier between each section. (Alternatively, line three 15cm tins.)

Mix together the butter and sugar in a large bowl until soft and pale. Add the eggs one at a time and beat together, then mix in the flour until combined and fluffy.

Divide the mixture into three bowls. Add a couple of drops of rose water and pink food gel to one bowl and fold through until pink. In the second bowl, add the lemon zest and juice and a little yellow colouring and mix through. In the third bowl, mix in the amaretto.

Continued overleaf →

Place each mixture in a separate section of the baking tray and bake for 20–30 minutes until risen, golden and springy to the touch.

Remove from oven and leave to cool slightly before turning the cakes out of the tray – you may need to use a sharp knife to loosen the edges. Transfer to a wire rack to cool completely.

To make the buttercream, whip together the butter and icing sugar until combined, then add a dash of cream and whip until light and fluffy and there are no grainy bits when you rub your fingers together.

To layer the cake, spread a little jam over the white amaretto sponge, then a 3–4mm layer of the buttercream over the yellow sponge. Place the yellow sponge on top of the white sponge, iced-side down. Spread a thin layer of jam on top of the yellow sponge and then the remaining buttercream over the pink sponge. Place the pink sponge on top of the yellow sponge, iced-side down.

With a very sharp knife, trim the edges so you have clean, sharp edges on each side. Dust the top with icing sugar and serve in THICK slices.

Store any leftover jam in a sterilised jar and in the fridge for up to two weeks. The cake will keep wrapped in an airtight container for up to three days.

Cherry + almond spotted dick

SERVES 6–8

225g self-raising flour
25g ground almonds
125g suet
75g golden caster sugar
pinch of salt
zest of 1 lemon
175g dried cherries
50g toasted flaked almonds,
    roughly chopped
150ml whole milk
knob of butter, for greasing
75g cherry jam

Spotted dick always raises a giggle! Even better when served or said at school, this is another proper nostalgic pudding. Raisins can get a bit boring, so I've made this almost Bakewell-esque version with cherries and almonds. The hot jammy centre is a lovely little surprise. You can change the fruits and nuts to suit your taste or what you have in your cupboards. Apple, sultana and cinnamon or cranberry and orange, or even white chocolate and dried strawberries are great combinations to mess with tradition! I serve my pudding with custard, but cream or ice cream work too.

Mix the flour, ground almonds, suet, sugar, salt and lemon zest together in a large bowl. Stir through the cherries and flaked almonds so they are covered in flour (you may need to chop the cherries slightly if they are too big). Pour in the milk and mix – but not too much. You need a firm but moist dough – add a few drops of water if it's looking too dry.

Grease a ceramic heatproof pudding basin or a 900g loaf tin with butter.

Pour the majority of the mixture into the pudding basin, make a hole in the middle and fill it with the jam. Cover the jam hole with the remaining mixture.

Make a loose fold/flap in a piece of greaseproof paper (so if the pudding grows and expands, so will the paper) and lay over the top of the pudding basin. Secure with a piece of string. Then do exactly the same with a piece of foil – making an almost tent shape so the pudding and greaseproof paper have space to grow. Secure tightly with string.

Place the pudding basin in a large saucepan and fill with water up to just under three quarters of the way up the bowl (under the string and greaseproof paper/foil). Cover the pan with a lid, bring to the boil and simmer for 1 hour to 1 hour 20 minutes. The pudding should be springy to touch.

Remove the basin from the water very carefully and leave to cool slightly before turning out and serving.

If using a loaf tin, it will take slightly less time as the pudding will be longer and thinner.

School dinner coconut + jam sponge

MAKES 9 'HEALTHY' SIZED SQUARES

100g desiccated coconut
160g golden caster sugar
160g unsalted butter
170g self-raising flour
½ tsp baking powder
3 eggs
zest 1 orange
splash of coconut milk
300g shop-bought or
    homemade raspberry jam
    (page 179)
custard, to serve

I think this might be my all-time favourite school dinner pudding. Another easy-peasy recipe that hits all the right spots – I know that this pudding makes people happy as I made and served hundreds of portions with hot vanilla custard during lockdown and everyone loved it. Sometimes just a little reminder or a memory is enough to make your day a little bit brighter. You can use whatever jam you like and flavour the sponge with zest or spices.

Preheat the oven to 160°C fan (180°C/350°F/Gas Mark 4) and line a 25cm square cake tin with greaseproof paper.

Scatter the desiccated coconut over a baking tray and toast in the oven for about 3-5 minutes until starting to turn golden brown. Set aside.

Put the sugar, butter, flour, baking powder, eggs, orange zest and coconut milk in a large bowl and, using an electric mixer or hand mixer, mix together until pale, fluffy and completely combined. Pour into the prepared tin and level out. Bake for 20–25 minutes until risen and golden brown or a skewer inserted into the centre comes out clean. Turn out on to a wire rack and leave to cool completely.

Spread the jam all over the cooled sponge – get right into the edges. Evenly sprinkle over the toasted desiccated coconut. Cut into squares and serve hot with custard.

Chocolate + apricot sponge with chocolate custard

MAKES ABOUT 9 PORTIONS

SPONGE:
110ml hot whole milk
100g milk or dark chocolate chips or milk or dark chocolate (minimum 70% cocoa solids), chopped into small pieces
225g golden caster sugar
250g unsalted butter, softened
4 eggs
225g self-raising flour
½ tsp baking powder
50g cocoa powder
150g dried apricots, chopped

I don't know if I've ever mentioned it, but I am a pudding fiend! I always have been, ever since school. Chocolate sponge with chocolate custard – if you don't remember this, then you get to try my version with sweet, chewy apricots that make an old faithful even more delightful.

Preheat the oven to 160°C fan (180°C/350°F/Gas Mark 4) and line a 25 x 38cm rectangular or similar sized square baking tin with greaseproof paper.

Make sure the milk is hot to the touch, then add the chocolate chips or chopped chocolate, stir and leave to melt.

Use either a free-standing electric mixer, handheld electric mixer or a wooden spoon (if you're working those muscles) to beat together the sugar and butter until whipped and pale. Add the eggs one at a time, beating between each addition until completely combined. Add the self-raising flour, baking powder and cocoa powder and mix until light and fluffy.

Mix the warm milk and chocolate until you have a hot chocolate consistency. Pour into the cake mixture and whip again until completely combined. It will look a little like chocolate mousse. Fold through the chopped apricots, then pour into the prepared tin and even out. Bake for 30–35 minutes until a knife inserted in the centre comes out clean. Remove from the oven and leave to cool in the tin while you make the custard.

CHOCOLATE CUSTARD:
300ml whole milk
200ml double cream
3 cardamom pods, squashed
1 egg
2 tbsp golden syrup
30g cocoa powder
pinch of salt
20g cornflour

To make the chocolate custard, pour the milk and cream into a saucepan, add the cardamom pods and bring to a simmer over a medium heat.

Meanwhile, in a large bowl, mix together the egg, golden syrup, cocoa powder, salt and cornflour until combined and slightly pale. Remove the cardamom pods and then pour into the sugar and egg mixture in a continuous stream, mixing constantly until completely combined.

Pour the custard back into the saucepan over a low heat and stir constantly until it has thickened and coats the back of a spoon.

Cut the warm sponge into big ol' squares and drench in the hot chocolate custard.

Come back for seconds...

Tiramisu bread + butter pudding with Baileys cream

SERVES 6

500ml whole milk
500ml double cream
1 tsp vanilla bean paste
2 eggs, plus 1 egg yolk
30g light soft brown sugar
250ml triple shot espresso
100ml Tia Maria
175g sponge fingers
  (ladyfingers)
50g unsalted butter,
  softened, plus extra
  for greasing
1 small loaf of sliced
  white bread
100 dark chocolate chips
25g demerara sugar
30g cocoa powder

**BAILEYS CREAM
(OPTIONAL):**
250g mascarpone
400ml double cream
50ml Baileys

Why have tiramisu or bread and butter pudding when you can have both together? These are two really retro puds that I've combined to make this delightful hot and stodgy dessert. I've kept the sponge fingers in there as they offer a different texture to the bread. Don't worry if you can't get hold of them though, just use extra bread or even try toasting a few slices.

To make the custard, heat the milk, 500ml cream and vanilla bean paste in a saucepan over a medium heat.

Put the eggs, egg yolk and light soft brown sugar in a bowl and mix together until the mixture starts to turn pale.

When the milk and cream mixture is just about simmering, pour it into the eggs and sugar in one steady stream, whisking constantly. Return the mixture to the saucepan over a low heat, mixing constantly until the custard starts to thicken very slightly.

Mix together the espresso and the Tia Maria and soak the sponge fingers in the mix.

Spread the butter over the sliced bread and cut each slice in half to form two triangles.

Grease a 30 x 25cm ovenproof dish with butter and add a row of bread triangles followed by a row of the coffee-soaked sponge fingers and so on, so you have a dish full of alternating rows of bread and sponge fingers. Sprinkle over the chocolate chips, then pour over the custard. If the custard has thickened up too much, you can mix in some more milk. Give the bread little bit of a push down so the custard gets in between all the layers. Set aside for 1 hour to allow it to really soak in.

Continued overleaf →

Preheat the oven to 160°C fan (180°C/350°F/Gas Mark 4).

Sprinkle over the demerara sugar and bake for 25–30 minutes until golden brown and bubbling.

Remove from the oven and set aside for 10 minutes while you make the cream.

Put the mascarpone, cream and Baileys in a bowl and mix together until you have a thick dropping consistency.

Serve a big wedge of the bread and butter pudding, topped with a dollop of the Baileys cream and a dusting of cocoa powder.

Fit.

Speculoos + jelly Arctic roll

SERVES 6-8

300g good-quality vanilla ice
  cream or gelato
200–250g crunchy speculoos
  biscuit spread (I used
  Biscoff)
10 raspberries
120g golden caster sugar, plus
  1 tbsp for dusting
4 eggs
120g self-raising flour
1 tsp ground cinnamon
200g shop-bought or
  homemade raspberry jam
  (page 179)
50g speculoos biscuits,
  crushed (I used Biscoff)

If you are going to have Arctic roll, make it this one. You don't need to buy the perfectly round, slightly powdery version because this is soft, a little spiced, fruity and has a speculoos centre running through the middle. You probably won't be able to get it perfectly round, I didn't, and that's fine. Use this slightly wonky, but completely delicious Arctic roll as a metaphor if you're ever feeling not quite 'perfect' – perfection doesn't exist, but this Arctic roll does.

Place the ice cream in the middle of a large piece of clingfilm. Squash the ice cream until about 25cm in length, then spoon the speculoos biscuit spread into the middle like a sausage and place the raspberries in a line on top. Now roll the ice cream up around the speculoos spread and raspberries by lifting the clingfilm up and over, fully encasing the spread in an ice-cream sausage. Gently roll into a smooth sausage, twist the ends of the clingfilm and transfer to the freezer to set.

Preheat the oven to 170°C fan (190°C/375°F/Gas Mark 5) and line a 30 x 24cm Swiss roll tin with greaseproof paper.

Whip together the sugar and eggs in the large bowl of a free-standing electric mixer, or using a handheld electric mixer, for about 5 minutes until tripled in volume, fluffy and light. This is called ribbon stage – when you lift the whisk out, the mixture should fall back in ribbons that sit on top of the mix for a few seconds. Gently fold in the flour and cinnamon in three batches, trying not to knock any air out of the mixture. Gently pour the mixture into the prepared tin and bake for 12–15 minutes.

Scatter the 1 tablespoon of sugar over a piece of greaseproof paper and carefully and quickly flip the cooked sponge over on to the sugar and remove the greaseproof paper. Very carefully roll the hot sponge up to cool completely.

Continued overleaf →

Once the sponge has cooled completely, carefully unroll it and spread over the raspberry jam.

Remove the ice-cream sausage from the freezer and place it in the middle of the jam-covered sponge. Re-roll the sponge up and around the ice cream, fully encasing it in the sponge. If the sponge is too big, then trim off any excess. If the sponge is too small simply slice off some of the ice cream. Gently roll the sponge in the crushed biscuits so they stick to the outside. Turn the Arctic roll over, so the join is at the bottom. Wrap in greaseproof paper and return to the freezer to set for a minimum of 2 hours.

Trim off the ends and serve in massive slices – should you have any left over, wrap it in greaseproof paper and keep in the freezer for up to a month.

Little taster treat for you!

Chocolate orange roly-poly with cinnamon custard

SERVES 6

butter, for greasing
175g self-raising flour,
    plus extra for dusting
25g cocoa powder
pinch of salt
50g golden caster sugar
zest of 1 orange
100g suet
150ml whole milk
7 tbsp good-quality
    thick-cut marmalade
100g dark chocolate
    (70% cocoa solids),
    finely chopped

Sweet but bitter marmalade and chocolate is a pretty beautiful match but feel free to experiment even more with this recipe. Try orange curd or milk chocolate if you've got a sweet tooth, or if you want to be traditional (or keep it simple), use the basic dough and just whack in a heap of jam. I promise you won't go back to Aunt-what's-her-name's version after trying this one!

Preheat the oven to 180°C fan (200°C/400°F/Gas Mark 6) and lightly grease a piece of greaseproof paper with butter.

Mix the flour, cocoa, salt, sugar and orange zest together in a large bowl. Stir through the suet until evenly mixed. Pour in the milk and mix together so you have a soft, but not wet dough. If it's looking too dry, add a couple drops of water.

Turn the dough out on to a lightly floured work surface and knead a little until it comes together. Roll out the dough to a rectangle about 20 x 30cm. Spread over the marmalade, leaving a 1cm border round the edge. Evenly sprinkle over the chocolate. From the short end, carefully roll the dough up like a Swiss roll.

Gently lift the roly-poly on to the middle of the greaseproof paper with the seam underneath.

Wrap the roly-poly in the greaseproof paper, but make a big enough fold or flap all the way along so the pudding can rise and grow and won't be restricted by the paper. Secure the ends tightly with string. Do exactly the same with a piece of foil.

Boil a kettle full of water. Place a cooling or roasting rack (something that will keep the pudding out of the water) on top of a tray and then fill the tray three quarters of the way up the sides with boiling water. Place the wrapped roly-poly on top of the rack and bake for 30–40 minutes until the roly-poly has risen and is springy to touch.

CINNAMON CUSTARD:
300ml whole milk
300ml double cream
1 tsp ground cinnamon
pinch of freshly grated nutmeg
25g golden caster sugar
3 egg yolks
2 tsp cornflour

To make the cinnamon custard, stir the milk, cream, cinnamon and nutmeg in a medium saucepan over a low-medium heat until just boiling, then reduce the heat.

Meanwhile, in a separate bowl, whisk together the sugar, egg yolks and cornflour until the mixture starts to turn a pale colour. Pour in the hot milk and cream in a slow and steady stream and whisk through. You might want to put the bowl on a tea towel or cloth to stop it moving. Keep pouring and whisking until all of the hot milk mixture has been incorporated. If you have any lumps, you can strain the mixture.

Pour the custard back into the saucepan over a low heat and stir constantly until the custard is thick and smooth and coats the back of a spoon.

Leave the roly-poly to cool slightly before unwrapping and slicing. Serve with the cinnamon custard.

There will be chocolate seeping out, but this is a very good thing!

Treacle, pecan + pear tart

SERVES 8

400g homemade or
shop-bought shortcrust
pastry
plain flour, for dusting
100g of bread (I used granary)
100g pecans
500g golden syrup
50g unsalted butter
1cm piece of fresh ginger,
grated
1 egg
50ml double cream
pinch of salt
2 pears (3 if small)
clotted cream, to serve

Try not to overfill the pastry case – it does bubble slightly.

A tongue twister and a cracking pudding. The blitzed pecans give this tart a really lovely texture and the pears cut through the sweet filling. Apples would work just as well, as would other nuts such as walnuts, Brazil nuts and even blitzed hazelnuts. Serve with clotted cream for a little difference.

Preheat the oven to 160°C fan (180°C/350°F/Gas Mark 4).

Roll out the pastry on a lightly floured work surface until about 4mm thick. Using the rolling pin, gently lift the pastry over the top of a 25cm loose-bottomed flan tin (or cake tin if you like a bit of depth). Gently ease the pastry into the edges, then prick the bottom all over with a fork. Leave a slight overhang of pastry.

Scrunch up a piece of greaseproof paper and guide into the sides of the pastry, then fill with baking beans or dried rice, beans or lentils. Don't forget to put the greaseproof paper in first! Bake for 15 minutes, then remove the greaseproof paper and baking beans and bake for a further 10 minutes or until just starting to turn golden.

While the pastry is baking, place the bread and pecans in a food processor or blender and blitz until you have coarse breadcrumbs. Put the golden syrup, butter and grated ginger in a saucepan and melt over a low heat until the syrup has become runnier and the butter has melted. Leave to cool slightly.

Once the syrup mix has cooled in the saucepan slightly, then crack in the egg and whisk through. Add the cream and mix again. Tip in the breadcrumb and pecan mix and add a pinch of salt. Mix through until evenly combined.

Peel and core the pears, then cut into thin slices.

Pour the breadcrumb syrup mixture into the blind-baked pastry case, then fan out the pear slices across the top. Place the tart on a flat baking tray and bake for 45–55 minutes (depending on the depth of tin) until the middle is just set.

Remove from the oven and leave to cool slightly. Using a sharp knife trim the edges of the cooked pastry so it is nice and even. Serve warm with a big dollop of clotted cream.

Toffee apples + pears

MAKES 4

2 ripe Conference pears
2 apples (I like Pink Lady)
225g caster sugar
2 tbsp golden syrup
25g unsalted butter
30g desiccated coconut
30g mixed nuts, chopped
  (or just hazelnuts are nice)
20g freeze-dried raspberries
50g dark chocolate (minimum
  70% cocoa solids)
50g white chocolate

Why do apples get all the crunchy caramel glory? Well no more, because just look at these beautiful, regal, pointy pears. It's also a little bit of cockney rhyming slang for you (just for you, Pop). And not just for Halloween either! You can play with toppings because as long as the caramel is still sticky, then you can stick whatever you want to it. Worried about your teeth? Then try dipping the fruit in melted chocolate instead.

Place the apples and pears into a jug of boiling water for 10–15 seconds and rub peel to remove any wax. Stick in a wooden stick through the bottom of each apple.

Put the sugar and 60ml water in a saucepan over a medium heat and heat until the sugar has completely dissolved. Add the golden syrup and butter and allow to bubble and heat up – do not stir. Using a thermometer, keep an eye on the temperature until it reaches 149–155°C (300–311°F) which is called the hard crack stage.

Lightly toast the coconut and chopped nuts either in a dry frying pan over a low heat or pop on a tray in an oven at 160°C fan (180°C/350°F/Gas Mark 4) for about 5 minutes and place in separate bowls to cool. Mix the freeze-dried raspberries with the coconut.

Once the caramel is at the hard crack stage, remove from the heat and allow the bubbles to disappear, then dip the apples and pears into the caramel, twirling them so they are completely covered.

Dip the top third of the apples in the toasted coconut and raspberries and stand on some greaseproof paper to cool and set. Dip the base of the pears in the toasted nuts, giving them a little nutty bottom, then set on the greaseproof paper to cool and set.

Melt both the chocolates in separate heatproof bowls either in 20-second blasts in the microwave or using a bain-marie, then drizzle the melted dark and white chocolate over the chopped nuts on the pears. Not just for Halloween.

Say it with cake

SWEET:

Chocolate, caramel and banana drip cake – 200

Blackberry and orange celebration cake – 204

Raspberry, blueberry and almond clafoutart – 207

Sherbet lemon cupcakes – 208

Fig and Brazil nut chocolate mud cake – 210

Lady Grey, orange and cranberry Belgian buns – 212

Pineapple, lime and ginger polenta cake – 215

Banoffee religieuse – 216

Peach and plum upside-down cake – 218

Double Decker brownie – 220

Rhubarb and lemon thyme custard trifle – 224

Tropical roulade – 227

Nectarine and fig galette – 229

Lemon, red grapefruit and coconut tart – 232

Blueberry and lemon macaroon tart – 234

Black forest millefeuille – 238

AT TIMES I need to bake, I have to bake. This chapter will consume you and take you to a little baking haven for as long as you need.

These bakes and cakes take time and effort and will reward you with wow-factor results – these are the sort of bakes that make me feel bloody good about myself and I know will make you feel good about yourself too!

They are not only lovely to look at, but taste even lovelier. Depression often means I am my own worst enemy and I don't feel good enough, I beat myself up when things go wrong, or I worry that something is my fault. Baking is one of the only things I feel good at and comes slightly more naturally to me, and when a recipe comes together brilliantly it gives me a little bit of light relief that is so needed on dark days.

I also love to bake for others. This chapter will include things you want to share with loved ones. We must look after ourselves as well as others, so treat yourself, and take your time making your bakes beautiful or simply sprinkle over some icing sugar and dig in with a fork or your hands!

Chocolate, caramel + banana drip cake

SERVES 12

CARAMEL SPONGE:
220g self-raising flour
150g golden caster sugar
50g light soft brown sugar
220g unsalted butter, softened
4 eggs
1 tsp baking powder
2 tbsp caramel
½ tsp vanilla bean paste

BANANA SPONGE:
110g self-raising flour
110g golden caster sugar
110g unsalted butter, softened
2 eggs
½ tsp baking powder
1 ripe banana, mashed
100g dark chocolate
    (minimum 70% cocoa solids),
    coarsely grated

Another big, beautiful cake with big, beautiful drips and ALL the chocolate. This was a little mix-up of a couple of different cakes I made, so I put them together and voila! Tried and tested on my Charby, and she bloody loved it. A drip cake is a great way to fancy up a cake without having to go all out on the decoration and you can also add broken chocolate, biscuits and more treats for added drama and sugar. Separate the cakes out and keep as one flavour if you must, but please make sure you enjoy a huge slice.

To make the ganache, pour the double cream into a saucepan over a low-medium heat until small bubbles break the surface. Remove from the heat and tip in the chocolate. Do not stir. Leave for 10 minutes, then mix through the chocolate until smooth and glossy. Set aside to cool.

Preheat the oven to 160°C fan (180°C/350°F/Gas Mark 4) and grease and line three 23cm loose-bottomed cake tins with greaseproof paper.

Put all the ingredients for the caramel sponge in a large bowl and either fit to a free-standing electric mixer or use a handheld electric mixer or a wooden spoon to mix until light, fluffy and combined. Divide the mixture between two of the sandwich tins, level out and bake for 20–25 minutes until risen, golden and springy to the touch. Leave to cool for 2 minutes, then turn out on to a wire rack to cool completely.

Clean out the mixing bowl and add all the ingredients for the banana sponge and, using your mixer of choice, mix until combined, light and fluffy. Tip the mixture into the remaining sandwich tin and level out. Bake for 20–25 minutes until risen, golden and springy to the touch. Leave to cool for 2 minutes, then turn out on to a wire rack to cool completely.

BUTTERCREAM:
250g unsalted butter, softened
725g icing sugar
1 tbsp toffee hot chocolate
   powder
2 tbsp caramel
175ml double cream

GANACHE:
200ml double cream
200g dark chocolate chips or
   dark chocolate (minimum
   70% cocoa solids), chopped

DECORATION:
5 tbsp runny caramel
50g dark chocolate (minimum
   70% cocoa solids), melted
100g banana chips
100g chocolate caramels

To make the buttercream, whip the butter in a large clean bowl using a free-standing electric mixer or handheld electric mixer for about 4 minutes until really pale and softly whipped. Add half the icing sugar and whip for a further 2 minutes. Add the remaining icing sugar, the toffee hot chocolate powder, caramel and 100ml of the double cream and continue to whip until you have a spreadable buttercream. This may take up to 5 minutes. You may need to add a little more cream – when you run the buttercream between your fingers it should feel smooth not grainy.

Spoon 1½ tablespoons of caramel on top of one of the caramel sponges and spread out, leaving about a 1cm border around the edge. Dollop on about a quarter of the buttercream and smooth out, trying to keep the caramel from seeping through. You need to make sure you have enough buttercream for the outside of the cake.

Spread a layer about 3mm thick of the cooled ganache over the banana sponge leaving a 1cm border around the edge. Turn the banana sponge over and place on top of the decorated caramel sponge, so the ganache-side is facing down. Spread another 3mm layer of ganache on top of the banana sponge, then another quarter of the buttercream and smooth out.

Spread another 1½ tablespoons of caramel on top of the second caramel sponge and turn upside down on to the decorated banana sponge.

✳ You should have the following layers: (1) caramel sponge, (2) caramel, (3) buttercream, (4) ganache, (5) banana sponge, (6) ganache, (7) buttercream, (8) caramel, (9) caramel sponge.

Continued overleaf →

Either transfer the remaining buttercream to a piping bag and pipe roughly around the outside or, using a palette knife, spread the buttercream directly around the cake and, using the palette knife or a cake smoother, smooth the buttercream evenly around the edge of the cake and across the top. At this point you will be able to see the sponges through the buttercream. Place the cake in the fridge for 30 minutes to set the crumb coat.

Remove the cake from the fridge and repeat the above step, completely coating the cake in buttercream and taking time to smooth out the buttercream around the sides and across the top. Return to the fridge to set.

Place the remaining runny caramel into a piping bag and cut a small hole in the bottom. Turning the cake as you go, drizzle the caramel around the edge so the caramel drips down the sides at different heights.

Repeat the step above with the melted dark chocolate in a piping bag, trying to get the drips in the gaps between the caramel drips. Place in the fridge so the chocolate and caramel drips set.

Transfer the remaining ganache to a piping bag fitted with a star nozzle (it should be set enough to pipe and hold its shape) and pipe little swirls on top of the caramel and chocolate all round the edge of the cake. You can do alternating heights if you're feeling fancy. If you have any buttercream left, you can do alternate buttercream and ganache swirls.

Top the swirls with the banana chips and broken chocolate caramels.

If you dip the palette knife in boiling water, you get a nice smooth surface.

Blackberry + orange celebration cake

**SERVES AT LEAST 12–15
HUNGRY PEOPLE**

ORANGE SPONGE:
450g unsalted butter,
    softened, plus extra
    for greasing
450g self-raising flour
450g golden caster sugar
8 large eggs
2 tsp baking powder
zest of 2 oranges,
    plus juice of 1
blue food colouring gel
yellow colouring gel
red colouring gel

DRIZZLE:
Zest and juice of 2 oranges
Zest and juice of 1 lemon
100g caster sugar

SWISS BUTTERCREAM:
6 egg whites
500g caster sugar
zest of 1 lemon
zest of 1 orange
500g unsalted butter,
    softened
orange food colouring

**FILLING AND
DECORATION:**
400g fresh blackberries

**If you are going to make a celebration cake, you may as well go big
and this is BIG. This cake kills two birds with one stone – it's a long
process so it keeps your hands and mind busy, but it's also a cake
that you would probably make for someone else, so it gives you
that little bit of gratification you often need from doing something
nice for someone. Change up the fruit (you can also swap it for
sweets) and colours to suit your mood or the celebration, and if you
don't want to go to the party or gathering, then that's OK too.**

Preheat the oven to 160°C fan (180°C/350°F/Gas Mark 4)
and grease four 20cm round cake tins and line the bases with
greaseproof paper.

Add all the ingredients for the orange sponge to the mixer and mix
until combined and fluffy – you may need to do this in two batches.
If so, just split the ingredients in half.

Divide the cake batter between four bowls and make one batch
yellow, one batch a pale orange, once batch pale red and the final
batch pale purple using the food colouring gels. Pour into the
prepared tins and bake for 20–25 minutes until risen and the sponge
is slightly coming away from the edges. Remove from the oven and
leave to cool for a couple of minutes, then turn out on to a wire rack
to cool completely.

To make the drizzle, put the orange and lemon zest and juice and
sugar in a saucepan over a low heat and allow the sugar to dissolve,
then bubble slightly to create a syrupy drizzle. While the four cakes are
still warm, poke a few holes in each and drizzle over the warm syrup.

To make the Swiss buttercream, mix together the egg whites and
sugar in a heatproof bowl set over a saucepan of simmering water
(a bain-marie) until the sugar has completely dissolved. Tip into
the large bowl and of a free-standing electric mixer and whip until
you have glossy stiff peaks. Add the zest and then, with the mixer
on a medium/high speed, add the butter one knob at a time until
completely combined and smooth. If the buttercream is too soft,
place in the fridge for 10 minutes at a time before re whipping.

Transfer three fifths of the buttercream to a piping bag and snip a 2.5cm hole in the end.

Place the yellow sponge on a turn table or on a display plate, then squeeze on one third of the buttercream, dot on some crushed blackberries and then top with the orange sponge. Repeat with buttercream and a few blackberries. Now add the red sponge and, using a long sharp knife, cut out the middle of the red and orange sponges so you have a hole. Fill with fresh blackberries, then spread over the remaining buttercream and top with the purple sponge.

Transfer half the remaining buttercream into the same piping bag and spin the four-layered cake around, squeezing icing as you go. Using a palette knife or an icing edger, create a crumb coating, smoothing the icing all the way around and over the top of the cake. Transfer to the fridge to set.

Divide the remaining buttercream equally between four bowls and add food colouring gel to make yellow, orange, red and purple icing. Using the back of a spoon or palette knife, smudge on all the different colours, swiping upwards, starting at the bottom and working up becoming sparser and more spaced out as you move towards the top of the cake. Top with a few blackberries and zest in a crescent shape.

This cake will keep for three days in an airtight container.

Dip the palette knife in hot water to get a really smooth finish

Raspberry, blueberry + almond clafoutart

SERVES 8

300g sheet of puff pastry
2 eggs
40g light soft brown sugar
25ml spiced rum
65ml whole milk
65ml double cream
zest of 1 lemon
sprig of fresh lemon thyme,
   leaves only (optional)
25g unsalted butter, melted
30g plain flour
200g fresh blueberries
200g fresh raspberries
30g flaked almonds
cream, to serve

What could be better than sweet batter spiked with fresh raspberries and blueberries? Sweet batter when it's being given a little hug by flaky puff pastry! Not totally authentic I know, but I couldn't resist. If you want to stick to the French way, then skip the pastry and pop the batter straight in a buttered tin. It's like the ultimate stodgy, sweet Yorkshire pudding.

Preheat the oven to 160°C fan (180°C/350°F/Gas Mark 4).

Gently lift and tease the puff pastry into the flutes of a 23–25cm loose-bottomed flan tin. Leave the edges sticking up and jagged, then gently squeeze and fold over.

Scrunch up some greaseproof paper and lay into the pastry case. Weigh down with baking beans or dried lentils or rice. Bake for 15 minutes, then remove the greaseproof paper and baking beans and bake for a further 5 minutes.

Beat the eggs, sugar and rum together in a jug. Then add the milk, cream, lemon zest and lemon thyme leaves, if using, and beat well. Pour in the melted butter and whisk vigorously. Sift in the flour and whisk until all the lumps are gone.

Tip the blueberries and raspberries into the pastry case and then pour in the batter. Scatter over the almonds and bake for 25–30 minutes until the batter is just set and starting to turn golden round the edges.

Remove from the oven and leave to cool until warm. Serve with pouring cream.

Best eaten on the day it's made, but any leftovers can be kept covered overnight in the fridge.

Sherbet lemon cupcakes

MAKES 18

220g self-raising flour
370g golden caster sugar
220g unsalted butter, softened
4 eggs, plus 2 large egg whites
   at room temperature
1 tsp baking powder
zest and juice 1 lime
6 tbsp lemon curd
yellow food colouring gel
18 sherbet lemon sweets
juice and seeds of 3 ripe
   passion fruit (optional)

Eat the cut-out bits as a little treat.

Cupcakes are just cheery little things. OK, these may not technically contain sherbet, but they look and taste lemony and zingy and they should make you pull that face when something is proper tart. Cupcakes are a really easy bake to adapt according to what flavours or fillings you want to use. You can use buttercream if you prefer, but I think the meringue makes these almost lemon-meringue-like and that can only be a good thing. Or take a trip down memory lane and make little wings out of the cut sponge for butterfly cakes, just like me and my Nan used to.

Preheat oven to 160°C fan (180°C/350°F/Gas Mark 4) and place cupcake cases into 18 muffin tin holes – you will probably need two muffin tins.

Put the flour, 220g of the sugar, butter, 4 eggs, baking powder, lime zest and juice in a large bowl and, using an electric mixer, mix until combined and fluffy. Fill each cupcake case two thirds full, then bake for 18–22 minutes until golden and risen. Remove from the oven and place on a wire rack to cool.

Once cooled, dig out the centre of each cupcake with a teaspoon and fill each one with 1 teaspoon of lemon curd.

Put the remaining 150g sugar and 60ml water in a saucepan over a low heat until the sugar has dissolved, then increase the heat to medium-high and allow to bubble away. Using a sugar thermometer, keep an eye on it until the sugar syrup reaches 116°C (241°F).

Meanwhile, whip the egg whites until they form fluffy peaks that hold their shape.

When the sugar syrup hits 116°C (241°F), very carefully and slowly drizzle the hot syrup down the edge of the bowl containing the whipped egg whites and whip continuously on a medium-high speed (do not pour the syrup on the whisk). Keep pouring the syrup in until it has all been incorporated, then continue whipping until the meringue is stiff, thick and glossy and the bowl no longer feels hot.

The meringue should be blood temperature by this point.

Add a round nozzle to a piping bag and paint a stripe of yellow food colouring down one side of the bag. Spoon the meringue into the piping bag. Pipe a rounded swirl of meringue on top of each cupcake (you should get a swirled yellow and white pattern). Use a kitchen blowtorch to lightly toast the meringue, then top with a sherbet lemon and a little drizzle of passion fruit, if using.

These will keep for up to two days in an airtight container.

Fig + Brazil nut chocolate mud cake

SERVES 8

150g unsalted butter, plus extra melted for greasing (optional)

150g dark chocolate chips or chunks of dark chocolate (minimum 70% cocoa solids), chopped

150g dark soft brown sugar

4 tbsp golden syrup

2 eggs

100ml hot whole milk

2 tsp good-quality instant coffee

20g cocoa powder

150g self-raising flour

pinch of salt

100g dried figs, chopped

100g Brazil nuts, chopped, plus a handful to decorate

3 fresh figs, quartered

GANACHE:

200ml double cream

150g dark chocolate chips or chunks of dark chocolate (minimum 70% cocoa solids), chopped

Clearly, I'm Bundt obsessed, but you can bake this in a standard tin you may just need to adjust the cooking times slightly – a loaf tin may take slightly longer than a larger, shallower tin which needs less time. The ganache is bitter and smooth, and the fresh figs look like regal gems sitting on top. They also remind me of my Grandad, who when I pulled out a mouldy satsuma from the back of the sofa (I don't know how it got there), was insistent that it was a fresh fig! This story makes my family smile a lot. Chop and change the nuts and dried fruit – date and macadamia nuts are good too.

Preheat the oven to 160°C fan (180°C/350°F/Gas Mark 4) and grease a 23 x 8cm rounded Bundt tin with melted butter or line a 23cm round cake tin with greaseproof paper.

Melt the butter and chocolate in a small saucepan over a low heat. Do not overheat as it will split. Remove from the heat when nearly melted and stir until glossy. Mix in the sugar and golden syrup, then – as long as the mixture isn't too hot – beat in the eggs.

Mix the hot milk, instant coffee powder and cocoa together in a jug and then mix into the melted chocolate mixture. Add the flour and salt and mix well until combined. Stir in the chopped figs and nuts. Pour into the prepared tin and level out. Bake for 30–40 minutes until a skewer inserted into the centre comes out clean.

Leave to cool in the tin for 10 minutes, then carefully turn out on to a wire rack – you may need to give the bottom of the Bundt tin a whack!

To make the ganache, pour the cream into a saucepan and heat over a low-medium heat until bubbling. Remove from the heat, add the chocolate and leave for 5 minutes, then stir until glossy. Leave to cool to a thick pouring consistency.

Use a chopstick or skewer to make some holes in the cooled cake and then pour over the ganache so it seeps into the holes and drips all over the sides. Top with the fresh figs and scattered nuts.

Lady Grey, orange + cranberry Belgian buns

MAKES 10-12

200ml whole milk
2 Lady Grey teabags, plus
   1 steeped in warm water
500g strong white bread flour,
   plus extra for dusting
1 tsp fine sea salt
2 tsp golden caster sugar
7g instant yeast
zest of 1 lemon
2 eggs, 1 beaten for egg wash
50g very soft unsalted butter
5 tbsp orange curd
125g dried cranberries, plus
   extra to decorate
125g macadamia nuts,
   chopped, plus 5-6 nuts,
   halved
200g icing sugar

I love admiring these through the windows of bakeries and then buying one and inhaling it. One thing I will never feel guilty about is having cake or buns and enjoying them. If something you eat makes you happy, then do it – everything in moderation. Life can be hard at times, so enjoy your buns! The making of this recipe is as therapeutic as the eating. It's up to you whether you cover these buns in thick white icing as they're good naked too.

Gently warm the milk and the teabags in a small saucepan and allow the teabags to infuse until the milk reaches blood temperature – if you dip your finger in you shouldn't be able to feel it as the liquid is the same temperature as your blood. Remove from the heat.

Put the flour in the bowl of a free-standing electric mixer fitted with the dough hook. Make a well in the middle and place the salt and sugar on one side and the yeast on the opposite side. Add the lemon zest. Crack the eggs into the well, remove the teabags from the milk and pour into the well. Mix on low speed until all of the flour has been incorporated, then increase the speed slightly and knead for 5–6 minutes. After about 4 minutes, add the butter in 3 batches until you have a smooth, stretchy dough.

If you want to make the dough by hand, knead for 9–10 minutes on a lightly oiled surface and build those muscles!

Shape the dough into a ball, tucking the seam underneath, place in a lightly oiled bowl and cover with clingfilm. Leave to rise in a warm place for 1½–2 hours until at least doubled in size.

Turn the dough out on to a lightly oiled work surface and, using your knuckles, knock the air out and then roll and stretch the dough. Roll out the dough to form a 25 x 45cm rectangle. Spread over the orange curd and sprinkle over the dried cranberries and macadamia nuts. From one short side, roll up like a Swiss roll, then slice into 10–12 buns with a sharp knife.

Line a large baking tray with greaseproof paper and space the buns out on the tray. Tuck the end slightly under each bun so that it doesn't unroll. Place in a large plastic bag, keeping the air in, and leave in a warm place for about 45 minutes or until doubled in size and springy when poked.

Preheat the oven to 180°C fan (200°C/400°F/Gas Mark 6).

Brush each bun with beaten egg and bake for 20–25 minutes until the buns have risen and are golden brown. Remove from the oven and place on a wire rack to cool completely.

Put the icing sugar in a bowl and add a teaspoon of the Lady Grey water at a time and mix until you have a smooth but thick drizzling consistency. Swirling and twirling, drizzle the icing all over the buns and top each one with a couple of cranberries and half a macadamia nut.

These are best eaten on the day but can be eaten the next day.

Try warming them!

I've made this
another Bundt, but
it works just as well
in a loaf tin.

Pineapple, lime + ginger polenta cake

SERVES 8

200g unsalted butter plus
   1 tbsp
plain flour, for dusting
   (optional)
100g polenta (fine cornmeal),
   plus extra for dusting
   (optional)
250g ground almonds
1½ tsp baking powder
pinch of salt
200g golden caster sugar
3 large eggs
zest of 2 limes
thumb-sized piece of fresh
   ginger, grated
300g fresh pineapple chunks,
   or tinned pineapple rings,
   cut into chunks

SYRUP:
50g caster sugar
juice of 2 limes

DECORATION:
100g icing sugar
2–3 tbsp juice from the
   pineapple chunks (if using
   tinned pineapple), or water
   if using fresh pineapple
zest of 1 lime
finely sliced pineapple chunks

Gluten-free friends, this one is for you should you wish to make it that way. It's all about the texture with this cake, slightly crumbly, almost gritty (in a good way), but also moist with lime drizzle.
You can use fresh pineapple or tinned – just be wary of the amount of juice. A little summery cake that can be eaten all year round to brighten up the cloudy days.

Preheat the oven to 160°C fan (180°C/350°F/Gas Mark 4) and brush a 23 x 8cm rounded Bundt tin with melted butter. Then dust with flour, or polenta for a completely gluten-free cake, shaking off any excess.

Mix the ground almonds, polenta, baking powder and salt together in a large bowl.

Mix the butter and sugar together in either a free-standing electric mixer or a large bowl with a handheld electric mixer or wooden spoon until light and whipped. Add the eggs and mix until combined. Add the lime zest, half the grated ginger and the polenta and ground almond mixture. Beat together until well combined. Fold through the pineapple chunks.

Tip the cake mixture into the Bundt tin and level out. Place the Bundt tin on a baking tray and bake for 40–50 minutes.

To make the syrup, put the caster sugar, lime juice and remaining grated ginger in a small saucepan over a low heat and let the sugar dissolve until you have a glossy syrup.

To check the cake is cooked, insert a skewer into the centre of the cake – if it comes out clean, it's ready. Remove from the oven and leave to cool for 5 minutes before poking holes all over the cake and evenly drizzling over the lime and ginger syrup until it is completely absorbed. Leave to cool completely.

Once cool, place a plate over the bottom of the cake tin and flip it over – the cake should drop out. Mix together the icing sugar and pineapple juice until you have a thick yet drizzly paste and drizzle all over the upturned cake. Decorate with lime zest and pineapple pieces. It will keep for up to three days in an airtight container.

Banoffee religieuse

MAKES ABOUT 8
DEPENDING ON SIZE

500ml double cream
3–4 ripe bananas
pinch of ground cinnamon
25g salted peanuts
handful of banana chips

CHOUX PASTRY:
55g unsalted butter
1 tsp vanilla bean paste
75g plain flour
pinch of salt
2 eggs

It should drop off a spoon slowly and hold its shape.

Little banana-y nuns. Fluffy, yet crisp choux filled with banana cream, caramel and topped with chocolate. These are quite the task, but once you've made them and adorned each one with a little cream collar and a banana crisp hat, the satisfaction is real! I've mentioned before my dad's love of anything cream-filled, so these are a dream pud or snack for him. Don't worry if they are a little out of shape, we all can be a little out of shape sometimes and that's just fine.

Preheat the oven to 190°C fan (210°C/410°F/Gas Mark 6) and line two baking sheets with greaseproof paper.

To make the choux pastry, put the butter, vanilla and 160ml water in a large saucepan over a medium heat and allow the butter to melt, then bring to a rolling boil.

Sift the flour and salt on to a folded piece of greaseproof paper.

When the buttery water is at boiling point, remove from the heat and in one go drop the flour into the water (I think this is called shunting!). Mix vigorously with a wooden spoon until the mixture leaves the sides of the pan and forms a soft ball in the centre. Return to a low heat and continue to stir the mixture for about one minute to cook out the flour.

Transfer the hot mix to a bowl and stir round and move it up the sides to help it cool down a little. When the mixture has cooled slightly, add 1 egg and beat using a hand-held electric mixer until the egg is incorporated and the mixture is starting to look thick and glossy. (It may look like it is curdling, but keep beating and it will come together.) Add the second egg and beat again until the choux dough is smooth, thick and glossy.

Spoon the dough into a piping bag and snip a 2cm opening in the end. Pipe out half the mixture into 4cm rounds (these will be the base) on to one of the lined baking sheets. Then pipe the remaining half into 2cm rounds (these will be the tops), leaving a little space between each one.

CARAMEL:
250g shop-bought caramel
  OR
75g unsalted butter
75g light soft brown sugar
75ml double cream

GANACHE:
200ml double cream
1 tbsp golden syrup
150g dark chocolate
  (minimum 70% cocoa solids)

Bake for 20–22 minutes for the smaller buns and 25–30 minutes for the bigger ones until golden, risen and crisp. Remove from the oven and transfer the choux buns to a wire rack to cool.

If you are making the caramel, put the butter and sugar in a saucepan over a low heat and cook until the sugar has dissolved, then increase the heat to medium and bubble away until frothing and bubbling. Remove from the heat and whisk through the cream. Transfer to the fridge to cool completely and thicken up. Then transfer to a piping bag and snip a small hole in the end.

To make the ganache, put the cream and syrup in saucepan and bring to a simmer with bubbles breaking on the surface. Remove from the heat, drop in the chocolate and leave for 5 minutes. Stir through until glossy and smooth and set aside to cool.

Whip the double cream until smooth, soft peaks form and transfer one third into a piping bag fitted with a star nozzle.

Mash the bananas roughly, then fold them through the remaining whipped cream with the cinnamon. Transfer to a piping bag and cut a 1cm hole in the bottom.

To assemble the religieuse, poke a hole in the top of the larger buns big enough to fit the end of the banana cream piping bag and squirt some banana cream inside. Squirt some of the caramel on top.

Poke a smaller hole in the bottom of the smaller choux buns and squirt in a little more of the banana cream, then add a little on the edge to use as a glue to stick to the larger buns.

Dip the top of the smaller choux buns in the ganache and place on top of the larger filled buns. You can alternate between placing the chocolate and caramel inside and on top for different variations.

Using the cream piping bag with the star nozzle, pipe little stars around the joins in the buns like little collars. Crumble some salted peanuts over the ganache and stick a banana chip on top of each bun.

Peach + plum upside-down cake

SERVES 6-8

115g unsalted butter, softened,
    plus 1 tbsp melted
115g light soft brown sugar,
    plus 2 tbsp
2 large ripe peaches
    (or tinned if you drain
    them well)
2 ripe plums
1 tbsp flaked almonds
90g self-raising flour
1 tsp baking powder
25g ground almonds
2 eggs
zest of 1 orange
pinch of fine sea salt

Peel the peaches if you're not keen on the fuzz or leave it on as it isn't too noticeable once the cake has cooked and the fruit has softened. A little tip – make sure you put the cake tin on a tray in the oven as if the fruit is super juicy, a loose-bottomed tin can leak and I for one hate cleaning the oven!

Preheat the oven to 160°C fan (180°C/350°F/Gas Mark 4).

Using a pastry brush, brush the tablespoon of melted butter all over the base and halfway up the sides of a 20cm springform cake tin. Sprinkle over the 2 tablespoons of sugar and shake the tin so that the sugar sticks to the butter.

Peel the peaches, cut in half, then remove the stones. Cut each half into three pieces and fan the pieces out on the bottom of the sugar-coated tin. Slice the plums in half and remove the stones. Then place the plums in between the peach pieces, flat-side down. Sprinkle over the flaked almonds.

Mix the sugar, butter, flour, baking powder, ground almonds, eggs, orange zest and salt together in a large bowl with a handheld electric mixer or wooden spoon, or in a free-standing electric mixer, until combined, light and fluffy. Pour the batter over the top of the arranged fruit and level out.

Bake for 35–40 minutes until golden and a skewer inserted into the centre comes out clean – remember the juices from the fruit will mean the sponge is a little more moist near the bottom. Tinned peaches may need a further 5 minutes cooking due to the extra liquid.

Leave to cool for 5 minutes, then place a plate over the top of the tin and quickly flip the tin over. Remove the cake tin so the peaches and plums now peek out on top.

Beautiful served warm with thick cream or cold with a hot cup of herbal tea.

It will keep in an airtight container for up to three days.

Double Decker brownie

MAKES 9 SQUARES

300g unsalted butter

275g dark chocolate chips
or 375g dark chocolate
(minimum 70% cocoa solids),
chopped*

125g light soft brown sugar

125g golden caster sugar

4 eggs

150g plain flour

200g nougat (you can use pink
and white, fancy ones with
nuts in, or whatever you like)

50g golden syrup

100g puffed rice (I used
Rice Krispies)

I had the opportunity to trek the Himalayas in 2019 with
CoppaFeel! and some of the most incredible people I have ever
met. People who have overcome illness themselves, or supported
family and friends through it, took on the challenge and crushed
it, all for charity. We were told to take snacks that would give us
energy on the long treks – I took about 30 Double Decker bars!
My goodness did it raise our spirits. So, I've turned the bar into
a brownie. This trip had a huge impact on my mental health –
standing on top of a mountain above the clouds knowing you have
accomplished something so few have, alongside real-life heroes,
changed my life. Team Candice, this one is for you.

Preheat the oven to 160°C fan (180°C/350°F/Gas Mark 4)
and line a 30–33 x 25cm rectangular or 28cm square tin with
greaseproof paper.

Melt 250g of the butter in a saucepan over a low-medium heat.
Remove from the heat and drop in the chocolate chips or 275g
of the dark chocolate – give it a jiggle so the chocolate is covered
in the hot butter and leave it for 2–3 minutes before giving it a
really good mix until smooth and glossy. If there are any lumps of
chocolate left, you can put the pan back over a low heat very briefly
until completely melted. Do not let the heat get too high or the
mixture may split.

*You can also replace
100g of the dark chocolate
with milk chocolate if
you like it a little
bit sweeter.

Mix in both types of sugar until just dissolved using a handheld electric mixer or wooden spoon. Make sure the mixture is not too warm – if it is, then leave it to cool. To speed up cooling you can transfer to a large bowl. Once cooled, add the eggs and mix fast and well. Fold through the flour until everything is combined into a smooth, glossy and chocolatey mixture. Pour into the prepared tin and smooth out.

Chop the nougat into bite-sized chunks and poke into the brownie batter, evenly spread out. Bake for 20–25 minutes until the top has a nice crack, but the underneath is gooey as anything and has a little wobble – like me! Leave to cool in the tin.

Put a saucepan of water over a medium heat and bring to a simmer, then place a heatproof bowl over the top, but make sure it is not touching the water. Add the remaining 100g dark chocolate (or 100g milk chocolate), remaining 50g butter and the golden syrup to the bowl and melt, mixing a little until smooth. Remove from the heat.

Pour the puffed rice into the melted chocolate and mix until they are completely covered. Pour the chocolate puffed rice over the cooled brownie and gently spread out so it is evenly covered. Leave to cool and set.

Slice into massive chunks and don't share! Any leftovers will keep in an airtight container for three days.

Image overleaf →

Rhubarb + lemon thyme custard trifle

SERVES 6-8

SWISS ROLL:
2 large eggs
60g golden caster sugar,
   plus extra for dusting
60g self-raising flour, sifted
finely grated zest of 1 orange
3 tbsp raspberry curd or jam

CUSTARD:
200ml double cream
200ml whole milk
zest of 1 lemon
small bunch of fresh
   lemon thyme
20g golden caster sugar
2 egg yolks
1 tsp cornflour

Rhubarb and custard anything for me please. The flavour, the smell, the gin. So how about getting together with some friends, having a good chat and sharing this stunning trifle with a big glass of gin and tonic, topped up with loads of ice, fruit and fancy paper straws? We need to talk more, reach out, share food, share drinks and share problems. It doesn't have to be with trifle, but it helps. If you can't get in-season rhubarb, try raspberries and strawberries or blueberries, or think ahead and freeze some rhubarb while it's in season.

Preheat the oven to 170°C fan (190°C/375°F/Gas Mark 5) and grease and line a 20 x 24cm Swiss roll tin with greaseproof paper.

Put the eggs and caster sugar in a mixing bowl and, using an electric mixer, beat for 5–6 minutes until doubled in volume and the mixture is at ribbon stage – when you lift the whisk out, the mixture should fall back in ribbons that sit on top of the mix for a few seconds. Using a large metal spoon, fold in the flour in three batches, making sure it is all incorporated. Add the orange zest with the last batch of flour. Pour into the prepared tin and spread evenly using a spatula. Bake for 12–15 minutes until just firm and light golden brown.

Place a piece of greaseproof paper on a work surface and sprinkle over some caster sugar. Quickly but carefully turn the sponge out on to the sugared paper. Peel away the greaseproof paper used to line the tin. Make an indent in the sponge about 2.5cm in, and then fold the edge of the sugared paper over the sponge at one short end, then roll up the cake with the paper inside. Leave the rolled cake to cool completely.

Once cooled, gently unroll and spread over the raspberry curd or jam. Roll back up so you have your filled Swiss roll. Set aside.

To make the custard, stir together the cream, milk and lemon zest in a medium heavy-based saucepan, then drop in the lemon thyme. Set over a low-medium heat and stir until just boiling.

RHUBARB JELLY:
600g rhubarb, chopped into
    3–4cm pieces
50ml rhubarb gin
120g golden caster sugar
5 sheets of leaf gelatine
200g raspberries

TO FINISH:
400ml double cream
white chocolate
sprigs of fresh lemon thyme

Mix the sugar, egg yolks and cornflour together in a bowl to make a smooth paste and whisk until the mixture starts to turn pale. Pour in the hot milk and cream in a slow steady stream and stir continuously until it's all incorporated. Pour the custard back into the saucepan over a low heat and stir until it is thick and smooth. Set aside to cool and thicken further.

To make the jelly, put the rhubarb, rhubarb gin, sugar and 75ml water in a saucepan over a medium heat and cook for 10–15 minutes until the sugar has dissolved and the rhubarb has started to soften.

Place the gelatine in a dish of cold water for 4–5 minutes to soak and soften. Once soft, squeeze out the excess water, add to the rhubarb and stir until dissolved.

To assemble the trifle, slice the Swiss roll into eight pieces about 4cm thick. Place the swirls of Swiss roll in the bottom of a trifle bowl (preferably glass if you have one).

Pour over the rhubarb jelly and drop in the raspberries. Transfer to the fridge to set.

Spoon over the lemon thyme custard, discarding the sprigs of lemon thyme.

Whip the double cream until soft peaks form, then transfer to a piping bag fitted with a star nozzle. Pipe small swirls on top of the custard with the central one slightly higher. Grate over some white chocolate and finish with a sprinkling of lemon thyme leaves.

Tropical roulade

SERVES 6-8

250g caster sugar
4 egg whites
zest and juice of 1 lime, halved
½ tsp cream of tartar
25g desiccated coconut
75g fresh or frozen (defrosted) pineapple, roughly chopped
75g fresh or frozen (defrosted) mango, roughly chopped
juice and seeds of 4 ripe passion fruit
150ml double cream
150ml mascarpone
50g white chocolate, melted
50g toasted coconut flakes

Summery, fruity and a little lighter than a sponge roulade, this one we actively want a bit misshapen with some cracks in as it adds to the character. Soft, chewy almost marshmallow-like meringue can be topped with whatever fruits are in season to put a smile on your face all year round. Try filling it with ice cream before serving and having a little baked-Alaska-type roulade – messy, but worth it.

Preheat the oven to 170°C fan (190°C/375°F/Gas Mark 5) and line a 20 x 30cm Swiss roll tin with greaseproof paper.

Scatter the sugar over a baking tray and place in the oven.

Wipe a large mixing bowl and the whisk attachment of a free-standing electric mixer with a lime half. Add the egg whites to the bowl of a free-standing electric mixer and whip until soft peaks form.

Remove the hot sugar from the oven and carefully, a spoonful at a time, mix into the egg whites until it is all incorporated. Whip until stiff, smooth and glossy and it's not grainy when you rub a little between your fingers. Add the cream of tartar and whip, then fold through the lime zest and coconut. Spread the meringue out evenly in the prepared tin. Bake for 25–30 minutes until very slightly golden on top and firm to touch, but still soft underneath.

Remove from the oven, leave on the greaseproof paper and place on a wire rack. Cover with a second piece of greaseproof paper and a damp tea towel and leave to cool completely.

While the meringue is cooling, mix together the pineapple, mango, passion fruit seeds and juice and lime juice.

Whip the double cream and mascarpone together until soft peaks form.

Continued overleaf →

Once the meringue is cool, flip it over and remove the tea towel and top layer of greaseproof paper. Spread over the whipped cream and swirl over the tropical fruit mix. If you have any fruit mix left, blitz to make a tropical coulis to pour over to serve.

Lift the greaseproof paper underneath the meringue and tuck the end of the meringue over and roll into a roulade/Swiss roll shape. The meringue will crack, but this is completely fine.

Drizzle over the melted white chocolate and sprinkle on the toasted coconut flakes. Pour over the tropical fruit coulis, if using.

Best eaten on the day – the meringue can be made a day ahead if left covered and then constructed a couple of hours before serving, but the fruit and cream may affect the meringue if left for too long. (They won't affect the taste though!)

Nectarine + fig galette

SERVES 6–8

3–4 nectarines
1 tbsp light soft brown sugar
1 tsp freshly grated ginger
zest and juice of 1 lemon
plain flour, for dusting
300g homemade or shop-
   bought shortcrust pastry
250g fresh figs
squeeze of honey
50g pistachios, chopped
1 egg, beaten
ice cream, to serve

A galette can be any number of things – a buckwheat filled pancake or a puff pastry wheel, but this guy is a lazy, scrunched-up edges tart filled with soft, in season nectarines and juicy, bursting figs. It's a quick and easy pudding that looks way fancier than it is. You can fill it with whatever fruit you want (just be wary of the amount of liquid) and serve in slices with ice cream, cream or custard. You can make mini ones too. Want a savoury version? Try feta and Mediterranean vegetables drizzled with balsamic.

Preheat the oven to 160°C fan (180°C/350°F/Gas Mark 4) and line a baking tray with greaseproof paper.

Slice the nectarines in half, remove the stones, then cut into small wedges. Put in a bowl with the sugar, ginger, lemon zest and juice and mix. Set aside.

Lightly flour a work surface and roll out the pastry to 3–4mm thick – a circle is great, but if it's a wonky square that's fine too.

Tip the nectarines into the centre of the pastry leaving about 4cm around the edge. Chop the figs into quarters and arrange these on top. Fold the edges of the pastry over so you have a circle with the fruit in the middle. Drizzle over the honey and sprinkle with the pistachios. Brush the beaten egg around the edges of the pastry and bake for 20–25 minutes until golden and the fruit is bubbling.

Remove from the oven and leave to cool slightly. Either cut into wedges and serve with ice cream or serve as a sharing pudding with ice cream dumped on top for everyone to dig in. Any leftovers will keep overnight in the fridge and can be warmed in the oven.

Image overleaf →

Lemon, red grapefruit + coconut tart

SERVES 8

PASTRY:
125g plain flour, plus extra
    for dusting
75g unsalted butter
30g icing sugar
50g desiccated coconut
pinch of salt
1 egg yolk

FILLING:
zest and juice of 2 lemons
juice of 1 large red grapefruit
    (if not particularly juicy you
    may need a second)
100g caster sugar
4 eggs
150ml double cream

TO FINISH:
75g coconut flakes
400ml double cream
150ml coconut cream

Hello, my beloved coconut. In this recipe it makes the pastry extra tasty and encases a smooth-as-silk lemon and red grapefruit filling. Like a tart au citron, but with red grapefruit bits. I did think about sieving the little bits out, but I really enjoy the little burst of flavour and pops of tartness. Make this whatever shape you like – a long rectangular tin means you get rectangular slices, which can look pretty cute. Dip your knife in boiling water before slicing so you get those sharp, clean edges.

Put the flour in a bowl with the butter and rub together with your fingertips until it resembles breadcrumbs. Add the icing sugar, coconut and a pinch of salt. Mix with your hands. Drop in the egg yolk and bring together using your hands. Add a teaspoon of water if the mixture is looking a little dry. Knead a little to bring the dough together, then flatten, wrap in clingfilm and transfer to the fridge to chill for 30 minutes.

Dust a work surface with flour and roll out the dough until about 3mm thick. Using a rolling pin, carefully lift the pastry up and over the top of a rectangular loose-bottomed flan tin. Gently push the pastry into the flutes using a little piece of pastry dipped in flour. Leave some pastry overhanging the edges. Prick the base with a fork and return to the fridge for 10 minutes.

Scrunch up some greaseproof paper and lay on top of the pastry. Weigh it down with baking beans or dried rice or lentils. Bake for 15 minutes, then remove the greaseproof paper and the beans and return to the oven for a further 5–6 minutes until the base is just starting to colour.

Reduce the oven temperature to 140°C fan (160°C/325°F/ Gas Mark 3).

Add the lemon zest and juice and the red grapefruit juice to a bowl, picking out any stray pips. Add the sugar, eggs and cream and whisk together until well combined. Pour into the pastry case (it may be easier to do this in the oven, so it doesn't spill – be careful not to burn yourself though!) Bake for 35–40 minutes until the centre is set.

Remove from the oven, leave to cool and trim off any excess pastry. Scatter the coconut flakes on a baking tray and toast in the oven for 4–5 minutes until golden brown.

Whip the double cream and coconut cream together until you have a soft piping consistency. Transfer to a piping bag and pipe little swirls along the length of the tart. Sprinkle with the toasted coconut flakes and serve. You can also just serve the tart, then whack on a lump of the coconut cream and sprinkle over the coconut flakes to serve. Any leftovers will keep in the fridge for up to two days.

Blueberry + lemon macaroon tart

SERVES 8

400g fresh or frozen
   blueberries
200g golden caster sugar
zest of 2 lemons and juice of 1
plain flour, for dusting
500g homemade or
   shop-bought shortcrust
   pastry
350g unsweetened
   desiccated coconut
1 x 397g tin condensed milk
4 egg whites

Another hybrid bake mixing two lovely things and making an even lovelier thing. I had a little disagreement about coconut with staff in the pub after they had the cheek to say Bounty had no place in a Celebrations box. Let me tell you, coconut has a place in my heart FOREVER! My sister Tan and my Mam are the same – we are all about the coconut. Soft, chewy coconut on top of tangy blueberry jam and crisp pastry turns a retro individual bake into a big banging pudding.

Put the blueberries, sugar, lemon juice and half the lemon zest in a saucepan over a medium heat and cook until the sugar has dissolved. Then increase the heat slightly so the fruit bubbles away for about 10 minutes. You don't want a really thick jam, more like a loose jammy blueberry sauce. Set aside.

Preheat the oven to 160°C fan (180°C/350°F/Gas Mark 4).

Lightly flour a work surface and roll out the pastry until about 3mm thick and large enough to fill a 28cm loose-bottomed tart or flan tin. Use the rolling pin to gently lift the pastry into the tin and, using a piece of pastry, guide the pastry into the flutes, then prick all over with a fork. Leave the pastry hanging over the top of the tin and place on a baking tray.

Scrunch up a piece of greaseproof paper and place in the pastry. Fill this with baking beans or dried lentils or rice. Place in the oven to blind bake for 15 minutes. Then remove the greaseproof paper and beans and return to the oven for a further 5–10 minutes until the pastry has just started to turn golden. Remove from the oven and set aside.

Mix together the desiccated coconut and remaining lemon zest in a bowl. Pour in the condensed milk and mix well.

In a separate clean bowl, whip the egg whites either using a stand mixer or a hand mixer until you have fluffy peaks. Fold the egg whites into the coconut mixture, trying to keep as much air in as possible.

Spread the blueberry jammy mixture across the base of the pastry case and then top with the coconut macaroon mix. Try not to squish out all the blueberry over the edges and create a little coconut mound in the middle. Bake for 20–25 minutes until the coconut mound has little golden jagged bits and you can just see some of the blueberry sauce bubbling round the edges.

Remove from the oven and allow to cool before removing from the tin.

Keep cool in the fridge for up to three days and rewarm in the oven, if you wish.

This is great served hot or cold. →

Image overleaf →

Black forest millefeuille

MAKES 5

500g block or roll of
    puff pastry
400g frozen black
    cherries, defrosted
100g golden caster sugar
50ml kirsch
zest of 1 lemon
400ml double cream
1 tsp vanilla bean paste
3 tbsp custard (if feeling
    decadent)
200g icing sugar
5 fresh cherries, to decorate

GANACHE:

150ml double cream
1 tbsp golden syrup
150g dark chocolate chips or
    dark chocolate (minimum
    70% cocoa solids), chopped

Fiddly to make and messy as hell to eat, but these are worth every single second, finger lick and cream splatter. I love looking at beautiful millefeuille in pastry-shop windows and will always buy one or three (for research purposes only!). These aren't too sweet as the bitter chocolate balances that gorgeous deep purple jam and sweet white icing. They are grown-up enough to serve at a dinner party or you can enjoy as a treat for one – just don't bother chopping the pastry and make a single giant version. Now that's what I call a treat.

Preheat the oven to 180°C fan (200°C/400°F/Gas Mark 6) and line a baking tray with greaseproof paper.

Roll out the pastry into a 20 x 30cm rectangle, 2–3mm thick. Place on the prepared baking tray and prick all over. Transfer to the freezer for about 10 minutes.

Place another baking tray or two on top of the pastry to help weigh it down and prevent it from puffing up too much during cooking. Bake for 15–20 minutes until golden brown and completely crisp.

Remove from the oven and, using a very sharp serrated knife, cut into 15 rectangles measuring 6 x 4cm. This will make five 3-layer millefeuille.

Put the cherries, sugar, kirsch and lemon zest in a saucepan over a low heat until the sugar has dissolved, then increase the heat slightly and bubble away for about 15 minutes until slightly reduced and thickening. Set aside to cool.

To make the chocolate ganache, heat the cream and golden syrup in another saucepan over a medium heat until almost boiling. Remove from the heat and drop in the chocolate. Leave for 5 minutes, then mix until smooth and glossy. Set aside to cool.

If using custard, add this before whipping.

Whip the double cream with the vanilla bean paste until soft peaks form. Transfer to a piping bag fitted with a star nozzle.

Once the ganache is cool, place three quarters in a piping bag and snip a small hole in the end.

Take one rectangle of pastry and pipe small stars of vanilla cream around the edge in a border. On the inside of this, pipe a second border of chocolate ganache and then fill the space in the middle with the cherry kirsch jam. Set a second rectangle of pastry on top and repeat with a star border of cream, then a border of ganache and then fill the centre with cherry jam. Repeat with the remaining pastry rectangles until you have five double-layered millefeuille and five rectangles spare.

In a small bowl, mix the icing sugar with a little water to create a thick but smooth icing.

Melt the remaining ganache so it is an easy piping consistency and place in a piping bag with a tiny hole in the end.

Spread the icing over the top of each of the remaining pieces of pastry until they are covered, then working quickly pipe straight lines of chocolate lengthways up and down the icing. Use a cocktail stick to drag the chocolate through the icing widthways to create a lovely feathered effect.

Using a palette knife, carefully lift each icing-covered piece of pastry on top of the double-layered millefeuille. Top with a fresh cherry and place in the fridge if not serving immediately. These will keep in the fridge for up to 24 hours, but bear in mind the pastry may become a little more soft.

Notes

I write all over my cookbooks and I'd love for you to be able to do the same. I know not everyone can bring themselves to scribble all over, so you can use these note pages to write down changes you make, new ideas and recipes, or anything you like!

Index

A

almonds: apricot + almond decorated biscuits 113
  cherry + almond spotted dick 181
  lamb, quinoa + feta 145–6
  peach + plum upside-down cake 218
  pineapple, lime + ginger polenta cake 215
  raspberry, blueberry + almond clafoutart 207
  white chocolate, cardamom, almond + lemon
    pastry twists 110–11
amaretto: apricot + almond decorated biscuits 113
  apricot + amaretto pastel de nata 121
American cheese: sausage patty breakfast bagels 167
angel cake 179–80
apples: apple + blackberry fool 36
  apple + pear sweet 'Dauphinoise' 125–6
  blackberry and apple jam 174
  crunchy coleslaw 80
  overnight porridge with apple, seeds + goji berries 154
  slow-cooked pork, celeriac + apple 147
  stewed fruit 155
  toffee apples + pears 196
apricots: apricot + almond decorated biscuits 113
  apricot + amaretto pastel de nata 121
  chocolate + apricot sponge with chocolate custard 184–5
  lamb, quinoa + feta 145–6
arancini (risotto balls) 74
Arctic roll: speculoos + jelly Arctic roll 189–90
artichokes: mushroom, artichoke + tarragon stroganoff 78
asparagus: goat's cheese, smoked salmon + asparagus
    filo tart 62
  Parmesan-crusted courgette + asparagus with tzatziki 21

B

bacon: bacon, cheese + chive croquettes 101–2
  the best potato salad 79
  croissant French toast 30
  everything-in Bolognese 60–1
  simple toastie 25
bagels: sausage patty breakfast bagels 167
Baileys + banana chocolate milkshake 46
Baileys cream 187–8
bananas: Baileys + banana chocolate milkshake 46
  banoffee religieuse 216–17
  chocolate, caramel + banana drip cake 200–2
banoffee religieuse 216–17

beans: smoky bean chilli 139
beef: everything-in Bolognese 60–1
  mozzarella-stuffed burgers + deep-fried pickles 87–8
  roast topside of beef 162
  slow-cooked beef brisket in ale 140–1
beetroot, feta + nigella seed scones 99
biscuits and cookies: apricot + almond decorated biscuits 113
  chocolate, orange + stem ginger shortbread 31
  oozy, gooey double chocolate one-pan cookies 32–3
  rocky road cookies 112
black forest millefeuille 238–9
blackberries: apple + blackberry fool 36
  blackberry and apple jam 174
  blackberry + orange celebration cake 204–5
  Tottenham cake 176
blueberries: blueberry + lemon macaroon tart 234–5
  raspberry, blueberry + almond clafoutart 207
Brazil nuts: fig + Brazil nut chocolate mud cake 210
bread: blue cheese, pesto + walnut bread 85–6
  chocolate caramel babka 123–4
  honey + lemon round challah 116–17
  khachapuri 92–3
  leek + potato soup with Stilton croutons 149–50
  tear + share turmeric, cumin + Gorgonzola bread 90–1
  tiramisu bread + butter pudding with Baileys cream 187–8
  see also toasties
Brie: brown butter macaroni cheese 164
broccoli: pork meatballs with creamy mustard broccoli
    + orzo 64–5
  prawn + chorizo fried rice 22
brownies: double-decker brownie 220–1
buns: banoffee religieuse 216–17
  Lady Grey, orange + cranberry Belgian buns 212–13
  Swedish cinnamon buns (Kanelbullar) 119–20
burgers: mozzarella-stuffed burgers + deep-fried
  pickles 87–8
burrata: chicken, sausage, butternut squash + burrata
  lasagne 56–7
butternut squash: cauliflower, squash, kale + cheese
    pasties 96–7
  chicken sausage, butternut squash + burrata lasagne 56–7

C

Cajun spice mix 68–9
cakes: angel cake 179–80
    blackberry + orange celebration cake 204–5
    chocolate, caramel + banana drip cake 200–2
    fig + Brazil nut chocolate mud cake 210
    gingerbread house 128–31
    peach + plum upside-down cake 218
    pineapple, lime + ginger polenta cake 215
    Tottenham cake 176
    tropical roulade 227–8
Camembert: khachapuri 92–3
caramel 217
    banoffee religieuse 216–17
    chocolate caramel babka 123–4
    chocolate, caramel + banana drip cake 200–2
    chocolate, caramel + chia seed rice pudding 156
carrots: crunchy coleslaw 80
    everything-in Bolognese 60–1
    lamb, quinoa + feta 145–6
    leftover turmeric chicken, pearl barley + mushroom
        soup 138
    roast topside of beef 162
    slow-cooked beef brisket in ale 140–1
    turmeric chicken + potatoes 136
cashew nuts: prawn + chorizo fried rice 22
    spicy chicken + cashew traybake 68–9
cauliflower, coconut + corn fritters 16
cauliflower, squash, kale + cheese pasties 96–7
celeriac: slow-cooked pork, celeriac + apple 147
celery: crunchy coleslaw 80
    everything-in Bolognese 60–1
    leek + potato soup with Stilton croutons 149–50
    leftover turmeric chicken, pearl barley + mushroom
        soup 138
    slow-cooked beef brisket in ale 140–1
Cheddar cheese: bacon, cheese + chive croquettes 101–2
    cauliflower, squash, kale + cheese pasties 96–7
    charred corn + smoked chilli cornbread 75
    pesto gnocchi gratin 67
    simple toastie 25
cheese *see* specific cheeses
cherries: black forest millefeuille 238–9
    cherry + almond spotted dick 181
chia seed: chocolate, caramel + chia seed rice pudding 156

chicken: chicken sausage, butternut squash + burrata
    lasagne 56–7
    leftover turmeric chicken, pearl barley + mushroom
        soup 138
    spicy chicken + cashew traybake 68–9
    turmeric chicken + potatoes 136
    ultimate chicken nuggets 50
chickpeas: coconut, spinach + pistachio chana dhal 153
    courgette, chickpea + halloumi falafel 100
    smoky bean chilli 139
chilli: smoky bean chilli 139
chocolate: Baileys + banana chocolate milkshake 46
    banoffee religieuse 216–17
    black forest millefeuille 238–9
    chocolate + apricot sponge with chocolate custard 184–5
    chocolate caramel babka 123–4
    chocolate, caramel + banana drip cake 200–2
    chocolate, caramel + chia seed rice pudding 156
    chocolate mint toothpaste 175
    chocolate orange roly-poly with cinnamon custard 192–3
    chocolate, orange + stem ginger shortbread 31
    chocolate sauce 39
    double-decker brownie 220–1
    fig + Brazil nut chocolate mud cake 210
    hot chocolate orange 45
    oozy, gooey double chocolate one-pan cookies 32–3
    rocky road cookies 112
    smoky bean chilli 139
    tiramisu bread + butter pudding with Baileys cream 187–8
    toffee apples + pears 196
    tropical roulade 227–8
    truffles 40
    whack-it-all-in chocolate cornflake rocky road 42
    white chocolate, cardamom, almond + lemon pastry
        twists 110–11
chorizo: everything-in Bolognese 60–1
    fancy eggs 14
    mozzarella-stuffed burgers + deep-fried pickles 87–8
    prawn + chorizo fried rice 22
    spicy chicken + cashew traybake 68–9
cinnamon: cinnamon custard 193
    cinnamon pastry twists with chocolate sauce 39
    Swedish cinnamon buns (Kanelbullar) 119–20
coconut: blueberry + lemon macaroon tart 234–5

cauliflower, coconut + corn fritters 16

coconut + lime scones 41

coconut, spinach + pistachio chana dhal 153

lemon, red grapefruit + coconut tart 232–3

mint chocolate & coconut truffles 40

school dinner coconut + jam sponge 182

toffee apples + pears 196

Tottenham cake 176

tropical roulade 227–8

cod: lemony tomato, pepper + cod parcels 54

Cointreau: hot chocolate orange 45

coleslaw: crunchy coleslaw 80

cookies see biscuits and cookies

cornbread: charred corn + smoked chilli cornbread 75

cornflakes: ultimate chicken nuggets 50

whack-it-all-in chocolate cornflake rocky road 42

courgettes: chicken sausage, butternut squash + burrata lasagne 56–7

courgette, chickpea + halloumi falafel 100

fancy eggs 14

Parmesan-crusted courgette + asparagus with tzatziki 21

slow-cooked beef brisket in ale 140–1

sweet potato + ham hock hash 172

cranberries: Lady Grey, orange + cranberry Belgian buns 212–13

stewed fruit 155

cream cheese: salmon + edamame bean fishcakes 107–8

croissant French toast 30

croquettes: bacon, cheese + chive croquettes 101–2

cupcakes: sherbet lemon cupcakes 208–9

D

drinks: Baileys + banana chocolate milkshake 46

hot chocolate orange 45

E

edamame beans: salmon + edamame bean fishcakes 107–8

eggs: the best hash browns – kedgeree style! 72–3

croissant French toast 30

fancy eggs 14

goat's cheese, smoked salmon + asparagus filo tart 62

khachapuri 92–3

sausage patty breakfast bagels 167

spinach, mushroom + blue cheese pancakes 26

sweet potato, garlic + red onion tortilla 53

sweet potato + ham hock hash 172

the ultimate toastie 25

Emmental cheese: brown butter macaroni cheese 164

the ultimate toastie 25

F

falafel: courgette, chickpea + halloumi falafel 100

feta cheese: beetroot, feta + nigella seed scones 99

lamb, quinoa + feta 145–6

figs: fig + Brazil nut chocolate mud cake 210

nectarine + fig galette 229

fish: proper pub beer-battered fish + chips with tartare sauce 168–9

see also cod; haddock; salmon

fool: apple + blackberry fool 36

French toast: croissant French toast 30

fritters: cauliflower, coconut + corn fritters 16

fruit: stewed fruit 155

G

ginger: chocolate, orange + stem ginger shortbread 31

pineapple, lime + ginger polenta cake 215

gingerbread house 128–31

gnocchi: homemade gnocchi 109

pesto gnocchi gratin 67

goat's cheese, smoked salmon + asparagus filo tart 62

goji berries: overnight porridge with apple, seeds + goji berries 154

Gorgonzola cheese: spinach, mushroom + blue cheese pancakes 26

tear + share turmeric, cumin + Gorgonzola bread 90–1

Gouda cheese: cauliflower, coconut + corn fritters 16

Grana Padano cheese: Parmesan-crusted courgette + asparagus with tzatziki 21

Grand Marnier: chocolate orange truffles 40

grapefruit: lemon, red grapefruit + coconut tart 232–3

H

haddock: the best hash browns – kedgeree style! 72–3

proper pub beer-battered fish + chips with tartare sauce 168–9

halloumi: courgette, chickpea + halloumi falafel 100

tortilla-crusted halloumi chips 17

ham hock: sweet potato + ham hock hash 172

hash browns: the best hash browns – kedgeree style! 72–3

hazelnuts: chocolate caramel babka 123–4

coffee & hazelnut truffles 40

herb + oat salmon fish fingers with tartare mayo 29

honey + lemon round challah 116–17

hot chocolate orange 45

J

jam tarts 174

K

kale: cauliflower, squash, kale + cheese pasties 96–7
  my type of pizza 104–5
khachapuri 92–3

L

Lady Grey, orange + cranberry Belgian buns 212–13
lamb: lamb, quinoa + feta 145–6
  roast lamb 161
lasagne: chicken sausage, butternut squash + burrata
lasagne 56–7
leeks: leek + potato soup with Stilton croutons 149–50
  pork meatballs with creamy mustard broccoli
    + orzo 64–5
  slow-cooked pork, celeriac + apple 147
lemon: blueberry + lemon macaroon tart 234–5
  honey + lemon round challah 116–17
  lemon, red grapefruit + coconut tart 232–3
  lemony tomato, pepper + cod parcels 54
  sherbet lemon cupcakes 208–9
  white chocolate, cardamom, almond + lemon
    pastry twists 110–11
lime: coconut + lime scones 41
  pineapple, lime + ginger polenta cake 215
linguine: everything-in Bolognese 60–1

M

macaroni: brown butter macaroni cheese 164
Manchego cheese: bacon, cheese + chive croquettes 101–2
  charred corn + smoked chilli cornbread 75
mango: tropical roulade 227–8
marshmallow: rocky road cookies 112
  whack-it-all-in chocolate cornflake rocky road 42
mascarpone cheese: pesto gnocchi gratin 67
  tropical roulade 227–8
mozzarella: arancini (risotto balls) 74
  khachapuri 92–3
  mozzarella-stuffed burgers + deep-fried pickles 87–8
  my type of pizza 104–5
  pesto gnocchi gratin 67
  sausage patty breakfast bagels 167
mushrooms: artichoke + tarragon stroganoff 78
  croissant French toast 30
  everything-in Bolognese 60–1
  fancy eggs 14
  leftover turmeric chicken, pearl barley + mushroom
    soup 138
  mushroom, spinach + sweetcorn risotto 148
  my type of pizza 104–5

pork meatballs with creamy mustard broccoli + orzo 64–5
prawn + chorizo fried rice 22
slow-cooked beef brisket in ale 140–1
spinach, mushroom + blue cheese pancakes 26

N

'nduja: fancy eggs 14
nectarine + fig galette 229

O

oats: herb + oat salmon fish fingers with tartare mayo 29
  overnight porridge with apple, seeds + goji berries 154
olives: everything-in Bolognese 60–1
  my type of pizza 104–5
  spicy chicken + cashew traybake 68–9
orange: blackberry + orange celebration cake 204–5
  chocolate orange roly-poly with cinnamon custard 192–3
  chocolate, orange + stem ginger shortbread 31
  chocolate orange truffles 40
  hot chocolate orange 45
  Lady Grey, orange + cranberry Belgian buns 212–13
orzo: pork meatballs with creamy mustard broccoli
  + orzo 64–5

P

pancakes: spinach, mushroom + blue cheese pancakes 26
Parmesan cheese: arancini (risotto balls) 74
  the best hash browns – kedgeree style! 72–3
  cauliflower, squash, kale + cheese pasties 96–7
  chicken sausage, butternut squash + burrata lasagne 56–7
  everything-in Bolognese 60–1
  fancy eggs 14
  herb + oat salmon fish fingers with tartare mayo 29
  mushroom, spinach + sweetcorn risotto 148
  spinach, mushroom + blue cheese pancakes 26
  tortilla-crusted halloumi chips 17
  ultimate chicken nuggets 50
passion fruit: tropical roulade 227–8
pasta: brown butter macaroni cheese 164
  chicken, sausage, butternut squash + burrata
    lasagne 56–7
  everything-in Bolognese 60–1
  pork meatballs with creamy mustard broccoli
    + orzo 64–5
pastel de nata: apricot + amaretto pastel de nata 121
pasties: cauliflower, squash, kale + cheese pasties 96–7
pastries: black forest millefeuille 238–9
  cinnamon pastry twists with chocolate sauce 39
  white chocolate, cardamom, almond + lemon
    pastry twists 110–11

peach + plum upside-down cake 218

pearl barley: leftover turmeric chicken, pearl barley + mushroom soup 138

    mushroom, spinach + sweetcorn risotto 148

pears: apple + pear sweet 'Dauphinoise' 125–6

    toffee apples + pears 196

    treacle, pecan + pear tart 195

pecans: treacle, pecan + pear tart 195

    whack-it-all-in chocolate cornflake rocky road 42

peppers: everything-in Bolognese 60–1

    fancy eggs 14

    lamb, quinoa + feta 145–6

    lemony tomato, pepper + cod parcels 54

    prawn + chorizo fried rice 22

    smoky bean chilli 139

    spicy chicken + cashew traybake 68–9

    sweet potato, garlic + red onion tortilla 53

    turmeric chicken + potatoes 136

pesto: blue cheese, pesto + walnut bread 85–6

    pesto gnocchi gratin 67

pineapple: pineapple, lime + ginger polenta cake 215

    tropical roulade 227–8

pistachios: apple + pear sweet 'Dauphinoise' 125–6

    coconut, spinach + pistachio chana dhal 153

    nectarine + fig galette 229

    oozy, gooey double chocolate one-pan cookies 32–3

pizza: my type of pizza 104–5

plums: peach + plum upside-down cake 218

polenta: charred corn + smoked chilli cornbread 75

    pineapple, lime + ginger polenta cake 215

pork: pork meatballs with creamy mustard broccoli + orzo 64–5

    roast pork shoulder with crackling 163

    sausage patty breakfast bagels 167

    slow-cooked pork, celeriac + apple 147

porridge: overnight porridge with apple, seeds + goji berries 154

potatoes: bacon, cheese + chive croquettes 101–2

    the best hash browns – kedgeree style! 72–3

    the best potato salad 79

    homemade gnocchi 109

    leek + potato soup with Stilton croutons 149–50

    proper pub beer-battered fish + chips with tartare \ sauce 168–9

    salmon + edamame bean fishcakes 107–8

    slow-cooked beef brisket in ale 140–1

    turmeric chicken + potatoes 136

prawn + chorizo fried rice 22

prosciutto: my type of pizza 104–5

Q

quinoa: lamb, quinoa + feta 145–6

R

raspberries: raspberry, blueberry + almond clafoutart 207

    speculoos + jelly Arctic roll 189–90

    toffee apples + pears 196

    Tottenham cake 176

raspberry jam 179

    angel cake 179–80

    school dinner coconut + jam sponge 182

    speculoos + jelly Arctic roll 189–90

red cabbage: crunchy coleslaw 80

red onions: sweet potato, garlic + red onion tortilla 53

rhubarb: rhubarb + lemon thyme custard trifle 224–5

    stewed fruit 155

rice: mushroom, spinach + sweetcorn risotto 148

    prawn + chorizo fried rice 22

rice pops: double-decker brownie 220–1

rice pudding: chocolate, caramel + chia seed rice pudding 156

ricotta cheese: chicken sausage, butternut squash + burrata lasagne 56–7

    croissant French toast 30

    khachapuri 92–3

risotto: arancini (risotto balls) 74

    mushroom, spinach + sweetcorn risotto 148

roast lamb 161

roast pork shoulder with crackling 163

roast topside of beef 162

rocky road: rocky road cookies 112

    whack-it-all-in chocolate cornflake rocky road 42

roly-poly: chocolate orange roly-poly with cinnamon custard 192–3

roulade: tropical roulade 227–8

S

salad: the best potato salad 79

salmon: goat's cheese, smoked salmon + asparagus filo tart 62

    herb + oat salmon fish fingers with tartare mayo 29

    salmon + edamame bean fishcakes 107–8

sausages: chicken sausage, butternut squash + burrata lasagne 56–7

    sausage patty breakfast bagels 167

    the ultimate toastie 25

school dinner coconut + jam sponge 182

scones: beetroot, feta + nigella seed scones 99

    coconut + lime scones 41

sherbet lemon cupcakes 208–9

shortbread: chocolate, orange + stem ginger shortbread 31

soup: leek + potato soup with Stilton croutons 149–50

    leftover turmeric chicken, pearl barley + mushroom soup 138

speculoos biscuit spread: rocky road cookies 112

    speculoos + jelly Arctic roll 189–90

speculoos biscuits: rocky road cookies 112

    speculoos + jelly Arctic roll 189–90

spicy chicken + cashew traybake 68–9

spicy sriracho mayo 50

spinach: chicken sausage, butternut squash + burrata lasagne 56–7

    coconut, spinach + pistachio chana dhal 153

    croissant French toast 30

    fancy eggs 14

    goat's cheese, smoked salmon + asparagus filo tart 62

    mushroom, spinach + sweetcorn risotto 148

    spinach, mushroom + blue cheese pancakes 26

    sweet potato + ham hock hash 172

spotted dick: cherry + almond spotted dick 181

stewed fruit 155

Stilton cheese: blue cheese, pesto + walnut bread 85–6

    leek + potato soup with Stilton croutons 149–50

string cheese: my type of pizza 104–5

stroganoff: mushroom, artichoke + tarragon stroganoff 78

swede: turmeric chicken + potatoes 136

Swedish cinnamon buns (Kanelbullar) 119–20

sweetcorn: cauliflower, coconut + corn fritters 16

    charred corn + smoked chilli cornbread 75

    mushroom, spinach + sweetcorn risotto 148

    prawn + chorizo fried rice 22

sweet potatoes: the best hash browns – kedgeree style! 72–3

    smoky bean chilli 139

    spicy chicken + cashew traybake 68–9

    sweet potato, garlic + red onion tortilla 53

    sweet potato + ham hock hash 172

Swiss chard: mushroom, spinach + sweetcorn risotto 148

T

tartare mayonnaise 29

tartare sauce 168

tarts: apricot + amaretto pastel de nata 121

    blueberry + lemon macaroon tart 234–5

    chocolate mint toothpaste 175

    goat's cheese, smoked salmon + asparagus filo tart 62

    jam tarts 174

    lemon, red grapefruit + coconut tart 232–3

    nectarine + fig galette 229

    raspberry, blueberry + almond clafoutart 207

    treacle, pecan + pear tart 195

tear + share turmeric, cumin + Gorgonzola bread 90–1

Tia Maria: coffee & hazelnut truffles 40

    tiramisu bread + butter pudding with Baileys \ cream 187–8

tiramisu bread + butter pudding with Baileys cream 187–8

toasties: simple toastie 25

    the ultimate toastie 25

toffee apples + pears 196

tomatoes: everything-in Bolognese 60–1

    lamb, quinoa + feta 145–6

    lemony tomato, pepper + cod parcels 54

    smoky bean chilli 139

    spicy chicken + cashew traybake 68–9

tortilla chips: sweet potato, garlic + red onion tortilla 53

tortilla-crusted halloumi chips 17

Tottenham cake 176

treacle, pecan + pear tart 195

trifle: rhubarb + lemon thyme custard trifle 224–5

tropical roulade 227–8

truffles 40

turmeric chicken + potatoes 136

tzatziki 21

W

walnuts: blue cheese, pesto + walnut bread 85–6

white cabbage: crunchy coleslaw 80

Acknowledgements

Flo, it's always you. I am me because of you.

Ironic that a book about food (my favourite thing) and mental health has nearly broken me. But in truth it has. This has been the toughest thing I have had to do. I have found it so hard to get things on paper. I am laying myself bare, talking about things I've not really spoken about and quite frankly I am terrified. But here it is, here is me and here is my food. All of it by me. I F'ING DID IT.

I can honestly say this year has been the hardest, most difficult, horrible year of my life. This book is testament to the fact that every day I just about put one foot in front of the other and I am here.

Mam and Pop, you are my reason for everything always. Would I ever think a year would pass without being able to hug you or think I would have to tell you things from the end of the driveway? But that's the way this year has been. Thank you for being my biggest fans, always on the end of the phone (even though I rarely answer) and for just being the best. A new knee and a pub extension all built in lockdown – you are actual superheroes!

Benj and Soph, you will never realise how much you actually kept me going this year. Our bubble. It was us three at one point and we did it. You checked on me, made sure I got out of bed, checked I was ok when I had a row with the fryer (said the C word) and you made sure I was never the third wheel. You kept me going – you really did, I don't know if I have said thank you enough. But thank you. I love you both very much – even though Albus loves you more than me, Soph.

Tan, Craig, Dan and Leslie. Good grief I love you all. I am shit, I know, but I know you are always there you bunch of funny buggers. Shit happens but we always have each other and Hey Vicky Vicky!

My Nan and Grandad and Nan Ivy. I think of you every day and know you would love this. It's smooth and perfect for a diet that's 98% Maltesers.

Matt, my gorgeous boy. I can't put into words how much your friendship means to me. You were put with me, but you have stuck with me. I am so proud of you, and can't wait to travel and cause mischief with you again properly. Never change my babe – know your worth.

Burnie and Charba – my girls. Without you I'm not sure what would have happened. The words I needed to hear when I couldn't think or find my own. Voices of encouragement, strength and pushing me on through voice notes, WhatsApp and pictures of those beautiful babies of yours, plus the socially distanced walks and cake exchanges. The pair of you are perfection in friendship form.

The Green Man Dem – staff who became friends. Taking the piss, understanding, testing my recipes, giving feedback and challenging me by being, at times, the naughtiest yet funniest people we could have working for us. We are still doing it; we are still here and still pushing forward. Stickers and all.

G, Anna, Kate and now Flo. Your trust and belief in me makes me (sometimes) believe in myself. You are not agents, you are family. I love you all very much, thank you for all you do and sorry for being constantly late with EVERYTHING!!!!

Frankie, you gave me the strength to do this. We met, became mates and now you are stuck with me. Thank you for giving me a little voice and making me feel brave.

When we spoke about a second book after *Comfort*, and I was asked about who I wanted to do photos, food styling and props... there was only one answer. You guys get my style completely. Ellis, now my mate and not just someone who takes the mick out my pie hole. You are so frigging talented and you even get me smiling now I have nice teef. Lou, you make my stuff beautiful when I can't and Hannah, one day, I'll sneak some of those stunning props out without you knowing. Thank you to Evie and Sophie for assisting Lou too.

Alice, you are an actual angel. The kindest of souls and you are a genius with a makeup brush. You are also my friend and I am very lucky for that.

Ebury team – Sam, Louise and Laura, thank you for allowing me to do this. You have seen me cry with emotion, and panic over this book, but THANK YOU for allowing me to be me and giving me my second book.

New friends and chefs allowing me in when I just fanny around with cake and becoming actual friends with my idols is mental. Thanks for letting me in and for all your help and advice. And you know what, sometimes my brownies really are as good as...

This is for every one of you who struggles, who gets surrounded by that grey cloud, for anyone who has stayed quiet through fear of being judged, questioned, or who has allowed mental health to get the better of them. This is for you. You are enough, you are ok, you can do it and in the words of this bake-off winner who in 2016 sobbed her heart out and said, "I'm good, I'm good enough" you are too, I promise and I'm here with you every step of the way. Never be ashamed of being you.

1

Published in 2021 by Ebury Press an imprint of Ebury Publishing,

20 Vauxhall Bridge Road,
London SW1V 2SA

Ebury Press is part of the Penguin Random House group of companies
whose addresses can be found at global.penguinrandomhouse.com

Copyright © Candice Brown 2021

First published by Ebury Press in 2021

www.penguin.co.uk

A CIP catalogue record for this book is available from the British Library

Project Editor: Sam Crisp
Photography: Ellis Parrinder
Design: Louise Evans
Food styling: Lou Kenney
Props styling: Hannah Wilkinson

ISBN 9781529108330

Printed and bound in China by C&C Offset Printing Co., Ltd

The authorised representative in the EEA is Penguin Random House Ireland,
Morrison Chambers, 32 Nassau Street, Dublin D02 YH68.

Penguin Random House is committed to a sustainable future for our business,
our readers and our planet. This book is made from Forest Stewardship Council®
certified paper.